Alvin Etler

late of Smith College

Making Music
an
introduction to
theory

 HARCOURT BRACE JOVANOVICH, INC.

New York   Chicago   San Francisco   Atlanta

ISBN: 0-15-554635-X

Library of Congress Catalog Card Number: 73-8589

Printed in the United States of America

Publisher's Note

The elementary writing discipline in this book is intended for first-year theory courses in colleges and music schools. No musical background is assumed other than that expected of all beginning music students—standard notation, scales and intervals, and meter. The course was developed during the years the author taught theory at Smith College, from 1949 until his death in June 1973. Alvin Etler was an eminent composer, but the course was equally successful in the hands of his noncomposing colleagues.

The emphasis of this book is squarely on writing, in a linear, tonal—though not diatonic—twentieth-century idiom that might be called "contemporary common practice." Although the approach is a genuinely creative one, it *is* a discipline: the students learn one-, two-, and three-part writing within a framework of rules governing the movement and relationship of tones—rules that are derived from the physical laws of the overtone series and are thus common to the music of all centuries. Only when the students are aware of the reasons for these rules, and have mastered their application, are they free to break them. In Etler's method there is nothing of the notion of composing as unrestrained "self-expression," with no criteria of validity except the students' taste.

Another requirement—stressed repeatedly throughout the book—is that the students write nothing that cannot be sung or played on the spot in class. (In Etler's own words to his students, "Live dangerously, but be sure you can sing it!") As a result, extensive practice in ear training, sight reading, melodic analysis—even rudimentary orchestration—occurs in the organic musical context of the students' own work, not as isolated drill for its own sake.

Obviously, *Making Music* presents a departure from the traditional emphasis of many theory programs on species counterpoint, fugal writing, and four-part harmonizations of Bach chorale tunes—techniques that teach students how composers of the sixteenth through nineteenth centuries dealt with musical materials, but that leave them ignorant of the practices of the composers of their own time. Theory instructors who are uneasy about this gap, but who until now have had no theory text to bridge it, will welcome the publication of this book. Once students have mastered the writing technique presented here, they will bring far more insight in subsequent courses to the techniques and styles of the composers of earlier centuries.

In a prefatory note to the manuscript of this book, the author extended his thanks to the members of the Smith College Department of Music for their indulgence "while for more than twenty years I have compulsively used their students for pedagogical experimentation." To those students he apologized for any deprivation along strictly conventional lines but trusted that his method offered them compensating rewards. Etler also acknowledged a former colleague, Professor Eugene Weigel of the University of Montana, as "a great teacher, who inadvertently taught me as well as his students. . . ." He went on to acknowledge the influence of *Exercises in Two-Part Writing* by Paul Hindemith, with whom he had studied at Yale. Of that book Etler wrote: "To my knowledge, it was the first book to systematically question the old pedagogical methods by suggesting that something more was needed."

Etler also extended special thanks to Professor Robert Miller of the Smith College Department of Music with these words: "Not only has he employed this discipline in his classes for over a decade, but through the years [his] innumerable discussions and constant corroboration of relevant pedagogical data have been indispensable." Alvin Etler died after the final version of his manuscript had gone to the typesetter, but before the galleys were ready. Therefore, the publisher also has special reason to be grateful to Professor Miller for his scrupulous reading of two stages of proof, particularly that of the musical examples.

CONTENTS

1 INTRODUCTION: THE RAW MATERIALS

THE OVERTONE SERIES

To compare the vast body of Western music in its astonishing variety with the meager physical phenomena which give rise to it is to gain a new respect for human ingenuity. Every use to which composers have ever put the element of pitch can be said to have its primary source in one simple property: the physical structure of a single tone—any single tone. If you have studied elementary physics, you will recall this structure as the *overtone series,* also called the harmonic series or the system of partials. Any vibrating body commonly used to produce a precise musical pitch—a string, a column of air, certain shapes of wood, metal, or membrane—exhibits this characteristic. As an example, consider the lowest string of the cello. It vibrates at the rate of 66 vibrations per second (66 Hz), producing the C two octaves below middle C. But simultaneously the string divides into two equal parts, each part vibrating twice as fast as the entire length—132 Hz. And at the same time, it divides into three, each of those parts vibrating three times as fast as the whole length—198 Hz. And at the same time, into four (264 Hz), five (330 Hz), six (396 Hz), seven (462 Hz), and so forth to infinity—way beyond the range of human perception. Example 1.1 is a pictorial representation of that vibrating cello C string, shortened and broadened for the sake of clarity, and for the same reason portraying the vibrations of only the first four partials, or divisions, of the string.

1.1

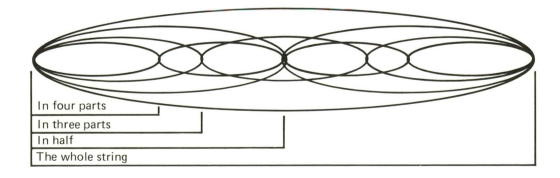

In four parts
In three parts
In half
The whole string

You can imagine how complicated the diagram would be if it were possible to include every one of the infinite number of divisions of the string—each with its separate rate of vibration. Yet a diagram that complicated would be necessary to represent the limitless number of separate frequencies, or pitches, that mingle to produce the surprisingly complicated sound we designate by the deceptively simple symbol ⸬.

Thus, when the C string of the cello is activated by the bow, or by some other means, it actually calls forth the aggregate of pitches, represented in Example 1.2 by the notational symbols most nearly approximating the actual frequencies. (It should be obvious

1.2

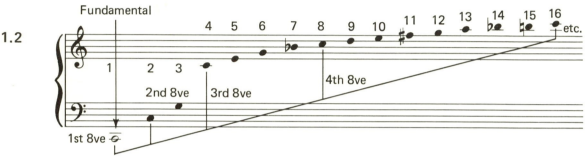

that if the fundamental generating tone were transposed to another note the entire series would be similarly transposed. Try writing out the series several times, each time on a different fundamental tone.)

These overtones are seldom, if ever, present in equal intensity. Various aspects of the vibrating medium—material, shape; size, surrounding material (as in the case of a column of air), method and means of activation, resonating chambers, etc.—bring about the intensification of some overtones and the suppression of others in an infinite variety of proportions. This variety is the principal factor distinguishing the sound of the human voice from that of the oboe, the flute from the viola, one clarinet from another, or even one instrument from itself in the hands of two different players. This function of the overtone series may not seem particularly important to you at the moment, but it could become increasingly so, particularly if at some time you find yourself working with a medium which allows you to control the structure of the tones themselves, such as the electronic synthesizer or, to an extent, the pipe organ. For now, familiarity with the series will serve as a means for you to understand why musicians have related tones to each other as they have, and why nature beckons toward the exploration of further relationships.

The overtone series is a bona fide phenomenon of the raw world of nature—the only such one in our experience with tones. A physical law ensures that a vibrating string in Bombay or Peking will produce the same superstructure as a similar string vibrating in Arezzo or Leipzig. Yet the perceptions aroused by the one in Bombay have prompted choices leading to a linear music with highly sensitive and well-codified microtonic divisions of the octave, which Western ears can hardly even identify, and to a heterophonic method of combining a melody with itself which takes little or no account of whatever tones may be sounding simultaneously. In contrast, the string vibrating in Arezzo spawned a tightly circumscribed system of chord structure and root sequence, together with a highly arbitrary, if thoroughly practical, division of the octave into twelve ostensibly equal intervals.

Surely neither of the arts born of our two hypothetical strings is superior to the other, or to other arts born of other strings. Each is merely the result of different perceptions drawn from the same natural phenomena. From this, one might very well be led to suspect that our Western art of tones consists of one immutable fact and a host of arbitrary decisions. For at any point in the chain of development, any number of factors —including chance—might have prompted a choice substantially different from the one actually made. One or more such alternative choices might very well have sent the art onto paths quite divergent from those actually followed.

Consider the analogy of the tree, which has long been one of the natural raw materials used in the making of everything from houses to the paper on which these words are printed. To work with wood, one must be thoroughly acquainted with its characteristics, possibilities, and limitations. A glance around you at almost any moment will reveal some of the myriad uses to which this material has been put and the proliferation of forms it has yielded.

So it is with music. We have seen how very little there is in the whole of the art which can truthfully be called "natural" in the physical sense. All the rest represents what composers have convincingly constructed from these few scraps of raw material. Thus the term "natural" as musicians tend to use it, though sometimes convenient, is misleading and confining. "Habitual" might be more accurate, since it conveys no more than the retention of aural patterns by virtue of repetition, and more readily indicates that those patterns are subject to change and replacement—as indeed they have always been. Those changes and replacements, together with the forces that bring them about, guided and restrained by common experience, have always been the lifeblood of composition and the essential concern of its students.

The assertion that the art has developed through a long sequence of arbitrary decisions in no way implies that that development has been haphazard. Quite the contrary! To shrink a long and complicated line almost to a dot: the history of Western music can be seen as a slow and arduous ascent of the steps of the overtone series. Beginning with the unison chant, the order in which the various intervals have been slowly and intuitively accepted as essential ones in the combining of simultaneously sounding voices has coincided generally, if not precisely, with that of their first appearance in the overtone series (Ex. 1.3):

Perfect unisons and octaves (chant—c. A. D. 600—900)
Perfect fifths and fourths (organum—to c. 1200)
Thirds and sixths (fauxbourdon—c. 1100—1300)
Sevenths, seconds, and tritones (the various seventh and
    ninth chords—from c. 1650)

1.3

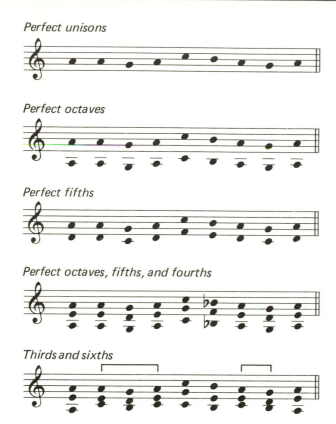

Perfect unisons

Perfect octaves

Perfect fifths

Perfect octaves, fifths, and fourths

Thirds and sixths

Furthermore, during the period of traditional harmonic practice (c. 1700—1900), chord roots progressed most often by fifths and fourths, less often by thirds, and least often by seconds. It is also to be noted that the Classical composers most often tended to consider those temporary tonal centers which were removed from the tonic by the distance of a perfect fifth (dominant and subdominant) to be the most closely related ones, those removed by thirds and seconds to be more remote, and the one removed by a tritone to be the most remote of all. The order of appearance of the intervals in the series is again corroborated.

The above, sketchy as it is, hints at the way musical usage has followed aural perception down through the centuries. But what of more recent practice? The traditional harmonic notion of chords consisting of superimposed thirds is, of course, inherent in the third octave of the overtone series. But what happened when the move up the series reached the fourth octave? We could project the answer from what happened after the ascent to the third octave: once the interval of a third had been accepted as a vertical relationship, then very soon the bare fifth of the second octave ceased to be used without the presence of a third. On the basis of that precedent, as musically perceptive ears probed beyond the third octave of the series, we could perhaps assume that third-constructed chords would soon be on the way out. That is precisely what occurred, about half a century ago, when Arnold Schoenberg spoke of the "liberation of the dissonance."

THE TEMPERED SYSTEM

Ever since late in the seventeenth century our instruments have been arbitrarily tuned according to a system called *equal temperament,* in which the octave is divided into twelve equal half-steps. The advent of this tuning method allowed the composer, for the first time, to move freely from one key to another—a novel impetus which made the enormous tonal developments of the eighteenth and nineteenth centuries possible.

Example 1.4a shows the twelve notes within the octave of the chromatic scale, placed equidistantly on the staff just as the tones are equidistant in the tempered octave. On the staff above the scale are the notes which approximate those of the fourth octave of the overtone series, spaced on the staff to represent their pitch relationship to the tempered tones.

1.4

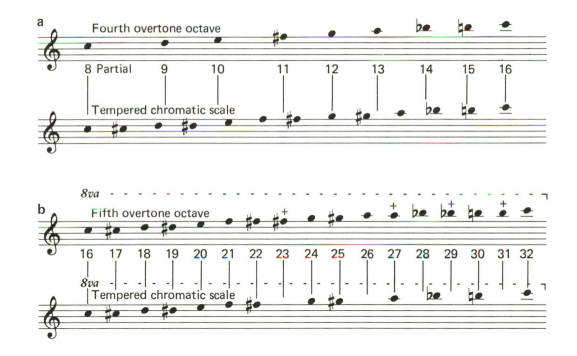

The third octave of the overtone series produced the common major triad C, E, G (partials 4, 5, and 6), and paved the way for the dominant seventh chord C, E, G, B♭ (partials 4, 5, 6, and 7). Example 1.4a demonstrates that while the fourth overtone octave produces the semblance of a scale, only a few of the tones more than approximate the tempered pitches. (A visit to a physicist could reveal the discrepancies in actual frequencies.) The fifth overtone octave (Ex. 1.4b) shows an even greater discrepancy between the series pitches and those of the tempered octave, especially in its upper reaches, where the tones of the series greatly outnumber those of the tempered scale, and the intervals between the tones are appreciably smaller than a half-step. Since the number of tones per octave doubles with each succeeding octave of the series, you can well imagine the cluttered appearance of a chart comparing the sixth octave with the tempered octave!

From these comparisons it seems evident that the tones of the tempered scale tend to lose their credibility as stand-ins for those of the natural frequencies of the fourth overtone octave. This condition becomes even more obvious in the fifth octave of the series. Twelve tones can hardly coincide with sixteen! Thus it would appear that our twelve-tone octave itself may be on the verge of obsolescence if our perceptions continue to probe and "climb" the series. Similarly, it might possibly be inferred that the two most prevalent as well as productive methods recently employed in dealing with pitch relationships —chance and twelve-tone serialization—are both avoiding the issue: the first by refusing battle and the second by pouring new wine (fresh perceptions) into old bottles (the tempered system). The past several decades have witnessed a number of comparatively isolated experiments with microtones of various sizes and derivations. Historical precedent would seem to suggest that these may very well be the harbingers of a genuine revolution in Western music—the first since the adoption of the tempered octave.

Since this book presents a simple writing discipline rather than a historical or scientific discourse, it is fervently to be hoped that your studies in these other areas will fill in the huge gaps left by this very brief description of a long historical line, confirm some of its speculations, and perhaps subject all these speculations to severe scrutiny. The purpose here is only to lay before you some evidence that learning how tones treat one another involves a great deal more than aping the patterns of any one moment in that historical line, regardless of how perfectly those patterns may have suited that particular moment. For tonal relationships are like living things: they have vitality only in growth and change. The writing discipline which you are setting out to master aims to prepare you for participation in that growth and change, whether as an active protagonist or as a satisfied supporting spectator.

SUGGESTED READING

John Backus: *The Acoustical Foundations of Music*
Howard Boatwright: *Introduction to the Theory of Music* (Appendix 1, "Notes on the Physics of Music")
Hermann L. F. Helmholtz: *Sensations of Tone*
Sir James Jeans: *Science and Music*
Jess J. Josephs: *The Physics of Sound*
R. Murray Schafer: *The New Soundscape*
Joseph Yasser: *A Theory of Evolving Tonality*

2 THE INTERVALS

This book assumes aural as well as notational knowledge and recognition of the intervals. Nevertheless, some discussion of their properties and use is called for, since a feeling for these properties and their exploitation is what music is all about—at least as far as pitch is concerned—and is basic to the chapters that follow.

TERMINOLOGY

We will use the traditional names for the intervals, simply because they are the ones in common use. As you proceed in the work, you will perhaps realize increasingly that their use is a compromise. The names spring directly from the modal-tonal use of seven-tone scales with five auxiliary tones (accidentals). In the present century the use of those scales has become so diluted as to render them virtually extinct. We are left with a system of pitch notation which admirably served the modal-tonal functions, but hardly expresses today's attitudes toward pitch relationships. Although more appropriate notational means already exist in response to the proliferation of new musical usages, they have not yet filtered down into common use; we therefore have little choice but to continue to use the system to which every practicing musician's reflexes are attuned.

The following abbreviations will be used:

P for perfect
M for major
m for minor
A for augmented
d for diminished

Thus P5 means perfect fifth, m3 means minor third, A4 means augmented fourth, etc.

A few definitions follow of terms which will be used often in this book:

Simple interval—an interval which spans an octave or less
Inverted interval—a simple interval whose lower tone has been transposed up an octave. (P5 inverted becomes P4; M3 becomes m6, etc.)
Compound interval—an interval which spans an octave plus a simple interval. (M3 compounded becomes M10; m6 becomes m13, etc.)

Harmonic interval—an interval whose two tones are heard simultaneously.

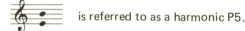 is referred to as a harmonic P5.

Melodic interval—an interval whose two tones are heard one after the other.

is referred to as a melodic P5. When an interval is used melodic-

ally, the relative durations can affect the aural impact of its characteristics, but not its *intrinsic* characteristics.

DERIVATION OF INTERVALS

Each of the common intervals shown in Example 2.1 has its prototype in the overtone series (Ex. 1.2). In general, the intervals which occur early in the series, close to the fundamental, exhibit more stability and repose than those more remote from the fundamental. Conversely, the intervals which first appear in the comparatively upper reaches of the series are characterized by greater restlessness or tension.

2.1

ROOTS OF INTERVALS

Now listen to the intervals. Play each one several times before going on to the next. Listen very carefully to determine which of the two tones, if either, tends to dominate the sound of the interval—possesses the greater stability—or, if you will, which is the "boss" or "tonic." Record your findings. Then double-check by repeating the process, but this time transpose each interval separately to a different tonal level in order to minimize any power the C might have gained through constant repetition.

> Stop at this point until you have accomplished to your complete satisfaction everything asked in the paragraph above.

Now, with your notes in hand, check against the following. Example 2.2 is the same as Example 2.1, but with the more stable tone of each interval indicated by an arrow. *Root,* not "tonic," is the term used for these tones.

2.2

P8 P5 P4 M6 M3 m3 m7 d5 m6 M2 A4 M7 m2

It will be noted that C is the root of any interval of which it is a member.* This is not surprising, since it is a very close relative, by octave transposition, of the fundamental C which generated the interval in the first place. The C does not dominate all those intervals in equal strength, but ranges from all-enveloping root power in P8 and P5 to only tentative strength in M2. Thus the dominance of the root diminishes with remoteness from the fundamental of the series.

In the cases of those intervals which do not contain a C, the dominance of the root is considerably less pronounced. Of M6 and m3 the E can and should be designated root, though there is a strong temptation to accept C as root rather than either of the tones of the interval. The sound of d5 and A4 is such that neither tone is stable or dominant, each actively seeking to move elsewhere. Therefore, no roots can be chosen. M7 is nearly as unstable as d5, because of the considerable tendency of both the F♯ and the G to move by half-step toward the octave transposition of the other. Any tone placed in surroundings which seem to impel its moving upward or downward by half-step (m2) is called a *leading tone.* The most common example is the seventh degree of the major scale, with its tendency to move upward to the eighth degree. A downward leading-tone tendency is exhibited by the sixth degree of the harmonic minor scale, which tends toward the dominant, and by the lowered second degree of any scale—for example, D♭–C in C major or minor. In M7, the G is designated root because of the added weight afforded by its registral placement on the bottom. In m2, the inversion of M7, that registral weight factor is lost, and it is very hard to justify a root designation of any appreciable stability.

We thus establish the *lower* tone as the root of P5, M3, m3, M7, m7, m9, and M9 (odd-numbered intervals); and the *upper* tone as the root of P4, M6, and m6 (even-numbered intervals). The upper tone is also more often than not the root of M2 (another even-numbered interval), though musical context can very easily reverse the roles, since the eighth partial in the series is flanked by two adjacent major seconds which make the choice difficult. The minor second is even more ambiguous as to root, since its first appearance in the overtone series is more remote from the fundamental than that of any other interval (partials 11 and 12). Furthermore, only on its second appearance does it contain an octave transposition of the fundamental.

*Remember that if the fundamental were some tone other than C, the whole series—all intervals, all relationships, and all roots—would be correspondingly transposed. If D were the fundamental generating tone, for instance, the whole series would be transposed up a whole step and D would be the root of all intervals of which it is a member.

The above discussion accounts only for the roots of the simpler intervals—perfect, major, and minor. With the exception of A4 and d5, augmented and diminished intervals sound like other intervals when played or sung simultaneously *out of context.* Thus:

A1 = m2	A5 = m6	d8 = M7	d4 = M3
A2 = m3	A6 = m7	d7 = M6	d3 = M2
A3 = P4	A7 = P8	d6 = P5	d2 = P1

Again excepting A4 and d5, augmented and diminished intervals result from *enharmonic spellings,* often employed to simplify notation. For practical purposes, A♯ and B♭ are symbols for the same sound, so the m7 (C-B♭) becomes A6 when spelled enharmonically (C-A♯). The roots are determined as if these augmented and diminished intervals *actually were* those intervals whose sounds they so closely resemble.

TENSE INTERVALS

While listening to the intervals you no doubt noticed, even if perhaps only incidentally, that sevenths, seconds, and tritones (a term we will often apply to both A4 and d5 by virtue of their identical sound) are tense intervals. That is, at least one of the tones sounds active in its wanting to move to another tone, which would resolve the tension. We will shortly examine these tensions together with their most appropriate resolutions. Look first, however, at Example 2.3, which takes into account the above discussion of the interval characteristics and arranges the intervals from left to right in order of increasing tension (and, it follows, from right to left in order of increasing stability).

2.3

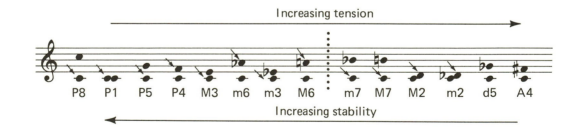

Compare this with the order of the appearance of the intervals in the overtone series (Ex. 2.1). M6 and m6 have been placed immediately after the thirds of which they are inversions because (other factors being equal) there is little difference in stability between these intervals and their inversions. Also, m7 and M7 have greater root stability than m3 and M6, but this is more than compensated for by the lack of active tendencies in the latter pair. M7 and M2 may perhaps appear to be reversed, but the greater root stability of M7, because of registral placement of the C, is here the deciding factor. P8 and its inversion, P1, could perhaps be omitted, since a single tone has little meaning without a context of other tones. They are included merely for the sake of completeness. A4 might also be deemed superfluous, since out of context its sound is identical with that of d5.

Only simple intervals have been discussed thus far. Compound intervals are considered to have the same characteristics as their simple counterparts—that is, M10 equals M3—except in the following instances:

1. If a root-position interval (root on the bottom) is stretched out to span more than an octave, the lower tone takes on even more strength as root.
2. If an inverted interval (root on top) is similarly stretched out, the upper tone is weakened in its perceptibility as root.
3. If a tense interval is thus stretched out, the tension is somewhat dissipated.

The sum of these three exceptions is that the lower a tone is placed registrally in relation to another tone, the more it tends to dominate. For instance, while the *upper* tone is the preferred root in M2, stretch it out to M9 and there is no question that the *lower* tone is root. (See the discussion of the relative stability of m2 and M7 on page 10.)

Perhaps you have noticed that in this discussion the terms "consonant" and "dissonant" have not been used, despite the fact that Example 2.3 shows, from left to right, the traditional four "perfect consonances," four "imperfect consonances," and six "dissonances." It is more practical for our purposes to consider the intervals from left to right in Example 2.3 as *gradually increasing* in tension while *gradually decreasing* in stability. Even in times of traditional harmonic practice, some perfect intervals were treated as more "perfect" than others, since parallel octaves were never permitted, and parallel perfect fifths were permitted only in very limited circumstances. On the other hand, parallel fourths could in some circumstances be used freely between upper voices, and the perfect fourth was even considered a dissonance at times. Similarly, the use of the major (or "Picardy") third to end pieces in the minor mode seemed to attribute greater consonance to M3 than to m3, while the various "dissonant" intervals have been traditionally described by such varying adjectives as "mild" (m7 and M2), "lush" (A4 and d5), and "sharp" (M7 and m2).

At this point it can be noted that the order of increasing *tension* as shown in Example 2.3 does not necessarily coincide with the increase in relative *harshness* of the intervals. The two terms must not be confused. The former conveys an active, dynamic quality which invites resolution. The latter describes a momentary impact on the nervous system. While the two are, of course, related, we are concerned first with the active role, or tension, of each interval, and how to handle it in context. Harshness has more to do with style and will be an important factor when we discuss the matter of prevailing sound.

RESOLUTION OF TENSE INTERVALS

More often than not, tense intervals require *resolution,* and the greater the tension is, the stronger is that requirement. In Example 2.4, resolution occurs, and is felt, when one of the two tones comprising an interval moves *by whole-step or half-step* to a third tone, which forms, together with the second tone, a new interval which is more stable than the original interval. (In the examples that follow, the moving tone of the first interval is labeled 1, the stationary tone 2, and the new tone of the second interval 3.)

2.4

One *restriction:* M2 and m2 never resolve to a perfect unison (Ex. 2.5). The plunge from rather high tension to its complete absence is too precipitous.

2.5

Throughout most of this work the intervals placed to the right of the dotted line in Example 2.3 will require immediate resolution. The two rules governing these resolutions are very simple:

    1. All sevenths and all diminished intervals resolve to a tone *within* the interval, as in Example 2.6.

2.6

Exceptions to rule 1:

    a. Because of the root ambiguities mentioned earlier and the leading-tone tendencies implied by the half-step motion (see page 9), M7 may resolve outward by half-step (Ex. 2.7).

2.7

    b. d3 resolves to an interval of greater tension (m2), as in Example 2.8. In order for tone 3 to be felt as the resolution, tone 2 must vacate the area by moving to a fourth tone (Ex. 2.9). This progression from tone 2 to tone 4 is free and is not to be considered in any way a part of the resolution—that being adequately accomplished by tone 3. (*Note:* All diminished intervals are considered, *in context,* to be intervals of tension, regardless of the fact that they may sound like other, simpler, intervals. They are resolved accordingly.)

2.8

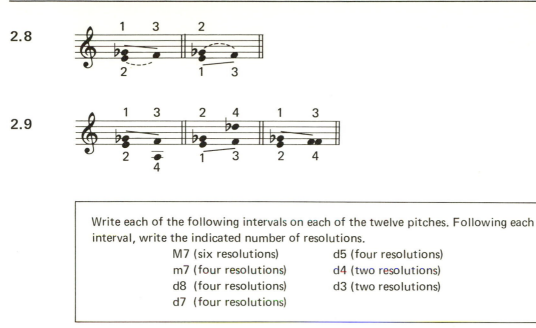

2.9

Write each of the following intervals on each of the twelve pitches. Following each interval, write the indicated number of resolutions.

M7 (six resolutions)	d5 (four resolutions)
m7 (four resolutions)	d4 (two resolutions)
d8 (four resolutions)	d3 (two resolutions)
d7 (four resolutions)	

2. All seconds and all augmented intervals resolve to a tone *outside* the interval, as in Example 2.10. (*Note:* All augmented intervals are considered, *in context,* to be intervals of tension, regardless of the fact that they may sound like other, simpler, intervals. They are resolved accordingly.)

2.10

Exceptions to rule 2:

a. The upper tone of A4 may resolve by whole-step *within* the interval (Ex. 2.11). This implies a momentary attribution of stability to the lower tone of A4. In Example 2.12, note the somewhat less effective, if still acceptable, *outward* whole-step resolution of the lower tone of d5 (A4 inverted).

2.11

2.12

b. A6, like its inversion d3, resolves to an interval of greater tension (M7), as in Example 2.13. Tone 2 therefore moves on to a fourth tone, which is free—not part of the resolution (Ex. 2.14).

2.13

2.14

Write each of the following intervals on each of the twelve pitches. Following each interval, write the indicated number of resolutions.

M2 (four resolutions)	A5 (two resolutions)
m2 (four resolutions)	A4 (five resolutions)
A8 (four resolutions)	A2 (two resolutions)
A6 (two resolutions)	A1 (four resolutions)

The resolutions of compound intervals are identical with those of their simple counterparts (Ex. 2.15), except that all ninths may resolve to tones either *within* or *outside* the interval, as in Example 2.16.

2.15

2.16

Examples 2.7 and 2.16 reveal six instances in which tones 2 and 3 are an octave apart. Find them and check them. In these cases tone 2 must move to a fourth tone simultaneously with the resolution, as in Example 2.17, in order to avoid direct resolution into an octave, which would bring about overprecipitous dissipation of tension. (See Ex. 2.5, in which the resolution to a unison makes this effect even more pronounced.)

2.17

In most other cases tone 2 may or may not move simultaneously with the resolution (Ex. 2.18). (But see Ex. 2.9 and 2.14.)

2.18

*Note that the essential element of resolution is the decrease in tension between the interval formed by tones 1 and 2 and that formed by 2 and 3. Since the progression of tone 1 to tone 3 in most cases accomplishes this (see Ex. 2.9 and 2.14), it is immaterial whether the interval formed by tones 3 and 4 be one of high, low, or no tension.

Write the following intervals on each of the twelve pitches. After each one, write the indicated number of resolutions. Circle all instances in which tone 2 must move simultaneously with the resolution.

M9 (six resolutions)

m9 (six resolutions)

Throughout the history of the art until about 1900, when the period of traditional harmonic practice ended, resolutions which move downward by whole-step or half-step were favored above the others—at times exclusively so. Compare the resolutions shown in Examples 2.6 to 2.18 with the roots of the intervals in Example 2.3. The comparison will reveal that, in general, composers preferred downward resolutions because they were unwilling to "unseat" the more stable tone (root) of the interval by forcing that tone to resolve the tension presumably caused by the interloping "dissonance." All resolutions are now available to you, however, by virtue of the fact that the practice of composers over the past several decades has been to place progressively less importance on roots or patterns of root sequence. Nevertheless, it is worth bearing in mind that the roots in Example 2.3 spring from the acoustical phenomenon of the overtone series as well as from habitual practice. Thus the upward resolution may of itself create a subtle kind of tension above and beyond the simple intervallic tension which it resolves.

RESOLUTION OF STABLE INTERVALS

The previous discussion has concerned itself only with the resolution of high-tension intervals (to the right of the dotted line in Ex. 2.3). The reason is that those intervals usually, though not always in the later parts of this study, require immediate resolution. Nothing has thus far been said about resolutions for those intervals whose tension is less marked (to the left of the dotted line). Because of their position in the series and because of cultural habit, we hear these intervals as inherently stable; thus they do not cry out for resolution and usually need none. There are situations, however, in which the composer can produce the effect of resolution: he can resolve one of these intervals to another of obviously greater stability (Ex. 2.19), or he can resolve to an interval so nearly similar in

stability that the second interval will be heard as a resolution merely because it is heard later—and perhaps for a longer time (Ex. 2.20). Context will have a great deal to do with the effectiveness of resolutions such as those shown in Examples 2.19 and 2.20. They will be effective only if surrounded by predominantly stable intervals.

2.20

At the moment, the material discussed in this chapter may seem to you somewhat disembodied. Beginning with Chapter 3, however, you will make it increasingly your own by putting it to ever more purposeful use. The application of these principles will become habitual to you, though your habits will change and be enlarged as you progress through this study and beyond. Composers today are very sophisticated in their attention to, as well as their apparent disregard of, these simple tenets. As you proceed, try to keep in mind that the elementary writing discipline set forth in these pages is based squarely on the assumption that no one, without exception, has ever achieved real freedom in musicianship or virtuosity in composition without first achieving genuine intimacy with the elemental functions of his raw materials.

SUGGESTED READING

Howard Boatwright: *Introduction to the Theory of Music* (Chapter 1, "Intervals")
L. S. Lloyd and Hugh Boyle: *Intervals, Scales and Temperaments*
Walter Piston: *Harmony* (Chapter 1)

3 THE MODEL

Models are short series of tones on which all our musical structures will be built. They are concerned exclusively with pitch relationships. Therefore, their tones are of indeterminate but equal duration, written in whole notes, as in Example 3.1. A good model is a sort of musical microcosm. It exhibits within its minimal dimensions many of the characteristics of a full-blown composition. It is tonally coherent and self-sufficient in that it has a point of departure, it departs, and it returns home. It maintains a sense of motion from beginning to end. It accomplishes this as gracefully and as interestingly as possible within its narrow limits. It brooks the presence of no idle tones whatsoever, and it insists that each tone jealously guard its independence, even while that tone contributes its maximum strength to the whole.

BOUNDARIES

In order to examine the nature of pitch relationships under the microscope, so to speak, we substantially avoid all other problems by keeping our musical structures very small. The model is, therefore, seldom more than a dozen tones in length, so that it will not become unwieldy. On the other hand, it should be not less than seven tones long. Though tonal coherence is possible with fewer than seven tones, the accomplishment of interest and grace within such narrow limits is most unlikely. Proportionally, its range will seldom exceed an octave, and then only by one or, at the very most, two tones. It should lie within the easy range of the normal untrained voice.

TONAL COHERENCE

Once the boundaries have been staked out, the next concern is tonal coherence. Clearly the first and most obvious step on the way to that coherence would be the establishment of one tone against which the functions of all the others are measured. Therefore, the model will return at the end to the same tone with which it began—in the same octave.

This tone is called the *tonic* and, depending on the functional measurements, it can be strong to the point of banality or weak almost to the point of extinction.

The first measurement comes with the choice of the penultimate tone. The melodic progression from this tone to the last should carry sufficient thrust to render the final tone creditable as the point of rest. So *if* that progression is by skip, as in Example 3.2, then the last tone must be the root of the interval skipped (never larger than P5). The approach to the final tonic may also be by step (M2 or m2), as in Example 3.3. In this case the condition of the final tone as root or nonroot of the final melodic interval is ambiguous and of no concern. This is amply compensated for by the melodic propulsion of the final stepwise progression.

A model

3.1

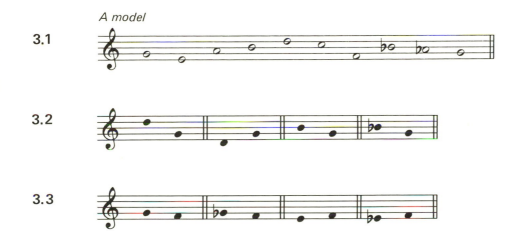

3.2

3.3

We have now established the point of departure and the return home. Between these two comes the departure, and it should be just that. We will, therefore, avoid any further emphasis on the tonic. Being premature, it would be disruptive. Therefore, avoid the tonic during the departure unless it is the second tone of a three-note scale passage (Ex. 3.4).

3.4

AVAILABLE INTERVALS

Still concerned with tonal coherence, let us look at the material available for the model. This consists of the twelve pitches contained in the octave and the melodic use of some of the intervals they form with one another. We freely use all the twelve tones because such use in composition has been virtually universal for well over half a century. In the interest of simplicity, melodic progressions are limited to perfect, major, and minor intervals (none larger than P5). For two reasons, this simplicity can be threatened by the use, *as melodic progressions,* of augmented and diminished intervals. The first reason is the ambiguity brought about by their aural identity with other, simpler, intervals, as discussed in Chapter 2 and illustrated in Example 3.5. The second reason is the contextual necessity for resolution of all augmented and diminished intervals (Ex. 3.6)—a necessity just as compelling when they are used melodically as when they are heard harmonically (review rules 1 and 2, pages 12-13).

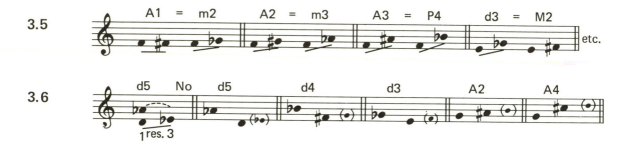

3.5

3.6

Ambiguity can, of course, be a powerful tool in the hands of a skillful composer, but in this instance its use in melodic progressions would undermine the simple tonal coherence sought in the narrow confines of the model. As for any tone requiring resolution, it is irrevocably bound to its two adjacent neighbors and they to it. This places *three* tones in an intolerable position for any tone which must jealously guard its independence. If you seriously question this, then take note of any sight-singing problems your class experiences when someone inadvertently includes one or two of these intervals in a model.

AUGMENTED AND DIMINISHED INTERVALS

Let me say again that the above discussion of available intervals refers to their melodic use only—the step or skip by which one note progresses to a second note. We have observed that augmented and diminished intervals have qualities which are undesirable in these melodic progressions. This does not mean, however, that we cannot enjoy the benefits of these qualities in the construction of the model. On the contrary, the very ambiguities raised by these intervals can be most useful. They can contribute to the strength of the departure. They can be powerful aids in controlling the strength or weakness of the tonal center. Finally, within the narrow scope of the model, they can lend a certain degree of expressive tension. Their use represents, in fact, a major area in the development of creative invention, skill, and control. We need only to know how to handle them. The model in Example 3.7 illustrates the proper use of no fewer than eight augmented and diminished intervals.

3.7

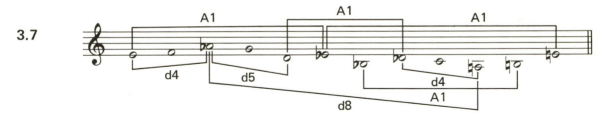

Another look at Examples 2.6 and 2.7 and the comments accompanying them will remind you that all augmented and diminished intervals demand resolution. You are also shown there how those resolutions are accomplished. We now come to the one basic rule governing the use of these intervals in the model: most augmented and diminished intervals may be used in the model if the two tones constituting the interval are tones 1 and 3 of a three-tone group and if tone 2 is the half-step resolution of the first tone (Ex. 3.8).

3.8

Some of the augmented and diminished intervals are not useful in this context because the resolution of the first tone necessitates the use of another such interval in progression from the second to the third tone, as in Example 3.9.

3.9

The diminished third is likewise eliminated because it produces still another ambiguity in the form of two successive half-steps. Successions of equal intervals (Ex. 3.10) tend to destroy tonal orientation unless the first and last tones of the group form a very stable interval, such as M3.

3.10

Because of the overwhelming stability of the skip between the first two tones, the two progressions in Example 3.11 may be employed provided that the three tones are not the last three in the model. Play or sing them for yourself. Why is the last tone unstable?

3.11

For the same reason the two progressions in Example 3.12 may be used. They may constitute the last three tones of the model provided that there is adequate support for the tonic elsewhere in the model.

3.12

The above discussion of the use of augmented and diminished intervals applies strictly to three-note groups. The rule decreases in rigidity as the number of intervening tones increases. Each case will be unique, and you will gradually develop judgment as to whether or not the ambiguity of the augmented or diminished interval has been dispelled by the intervening tones. In this respect, however, the augmented unison and the augmented and diminished octave are different from the others in that one of the intervening tones *must* be the one that resolves the first tone of the augmented unison or the augmented or diminished octave (Ex. 3.13).

3.13

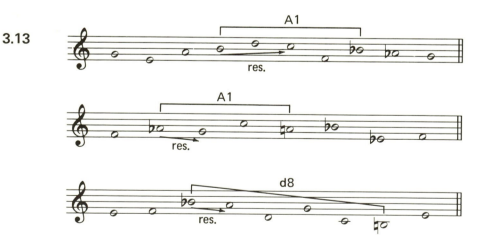

Exception: The first tone of these intervals may sometimes be resolved by a whole-step plus a half-step in the same direction before the appearance of the second tone (Ex. 3.14).

3.14

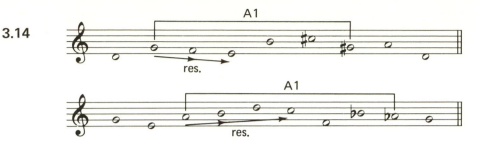

Though it is unlikely to occur with any great frequency, the use of the double-augmented unison, double-diminished octave, and double-augmented octave should be mentioned and illustrated (Ex. 3.15).

3.15

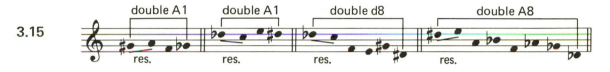

Another aspect of tonal coherence is the strength or weakness of the model's tonal center, which may be affected by the relationship between the tonic and the tones employed in the course of the departure. If a number of these tones are closely related to the tonic, then that tone's strength as tonal center is enhanced. The *perfect fifth* (dominant and subdominant) is to be considered a close relationship by virtue of its very early appearance in the overtone series. The dominant, a P5 above the tonic, exerts equal strength when transposed down an octave—P4 *below* the tonic. Similarly, the subdominant, or dominant (P5) *below* the tonic, exerts equal strength if it is transposed up an octave—P4 above the tonic. The *minor second* (either above or below the tonic) can be considered a close relationship because of its *melodic* strength as leading tone. Example 3.16* shows three models in which the use of these tones produces a strong tonal center.

3.16

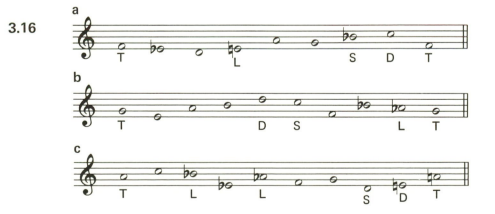

*In these and subsequent models, the following abbreviations are used: T—tonic; D—dominant; S—subdominant; L—leading tone.

If any of these closely related tones is also the root of a strong interval skip, the force of its contribution to the strength of the tonic is increased. In Example 3.17, such skips are marked, the letters above the staff indicating the functions of their roots.

3.17

In Examples 3.16a and c and 3.17, don't overlook the reinforcement lent to the final tonic by concentration of the subdominant and dominant functions close to that tonic.

The reverse of the above points is, of course, also true. If you deliberately seek a weaker tonic, use fewer of these functions and/or place them less strategically.

It must be pointed out here that, in a similar manner, the tones of the model might inadvertently lend support to some tone other than the tonic, as in Example 3.18. The model in this example is unsatisfactory. Though C is obviously the intended tonic, it has insufficient functional support to combat the overwhelming support for a hypothetical D♭ tonic. Play the model, omitting the first and last tones. It is pure D♭ major.

3.18

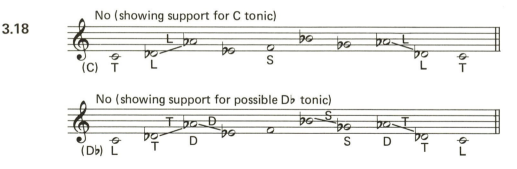

This kind of interaction of the various relationships within the model can be very subtle. Thus the balance of all the various factors can be a source of endless fascination and creative exercise.

SENSE OF MOTION

Vital as tonal coherence and control may be, they are not enough. A sense of motion is, of course, already present if we start with a tone, depart from it, and return to it. Such motion may be haphazard, however, and we seek to refine it, control it, and keep it constant. So we learn to avoid configurations which *ritard* (slow down) or interrupt the action. There are four of these configurations. Each of the first three tends to render a whole group of tones so helplessly dependent on one of its members as to make all but that tone virtually superfluous and idle:

1. The repetition of any tone before the intervention of at least two interval skips with two separate roots other than the tone repeated overemphasizes that tone

(Ex. 3.19). Even the intervening skips may not erase the ritarding effect of the repetition if the tone repeated has additional support outside or within the group (Ex. 3.20).

3.19

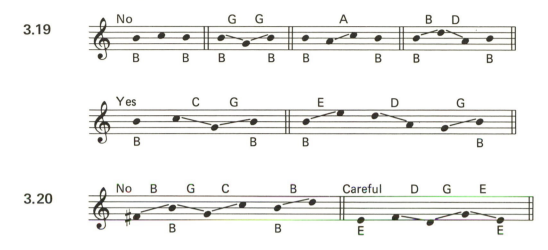

3.20

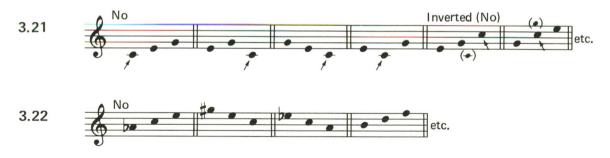

2. The formulation of conventional triads (chords consisting of two superimposed thirds) binds the members so inextricably to the chord root that all tones except the root are reduced to idleness (Ex. 3.21). Curiously enough, by virtue of habit, the same binding effect is produced even if the root of that conventional triad is ambiguous or nonexistent (Ex. 3.22).

3.21

3.22

3. Scalar passages render all but the first and last tones relatively meaningless. If such passages are limited to three tones, then only one tone is sacrificed. But this might turn out to be no sacrifice at all, for the tiny scale passage may lend a little grace by way of contrast. Scalar passages are therefore limited to three tones, and *must* be both preceded and followed by a change of direction lest the effect of a triad inadvertently hinted at (Ex. 3.23).

3.23

4. The fourth undesirable ritarding formulation is the sequence—repetition on a different tonal level of a two-or-more-note group (Ex. 3.24). Once a recognizable group has been heard, its repetition becomes redundant despite the different tonal level.

3.24

Two-note sequences are not seriously disruptive if there is only one repetition (Ex. 3.25).

3.25

It should be pointed out here that a model whose melodic progressions consist exclusively of alternating steps and skips, while not exactly sequential, does lose interest by virtue of its constant two-note grouping. This is particularly distressing if the skips are all the same size. In any case, the "step-skip syndrome," as in Example 3.26, is to be avoided.

3.26

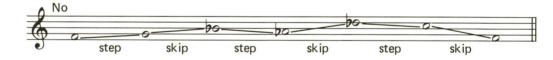

Strict avoidance of these four configurations tends to encourage a sense of motion but does not guarantee it. There are other, more subtle, ways in which motion can be impeded:

1. Emphasizing a simple triad by placing its members in the lower climax (lowest tone), upper climax (highest tone), and tonic positions (Ex. 3.27a). The same emphasis will result if upper and lower climaxes are an octave apart and if that tone is closely related to the tonic (Ex. 3.27b). This emphasis is greatly minimized, however, if there are other factors to balance its static effect, such as the avoidance of harmonic functional tones, particularly the dominant; a generous sprinkling of tones outside of any common scale; and several properly resolved augmented unisons, particularly if one of them involves the tonic itself (Ex. 3.28).

3.27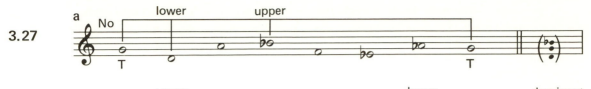

3.28

2. Including too many skips with the same root (Ex. 3.29). Note also the danger of repetition.

3.29

3. Not including a sufficient variety of intervals (Ex. 3.30).

3.30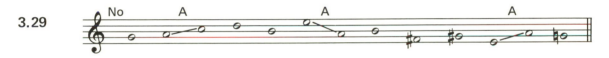

In writing your first models, you may very well find still more ways in which the motion can be ritarded! Only by a sustained effort to be acutely aware of precisely what happens in each of the models you write can you speed the arrival of that time when your instincts are so well developed that you can forget all about these rules. Then you can be confident that you and the tones are on terms so intimate that they will unresistingly do whatever you wish them to do.

GRACE AND INTEREST

We now turn our attention to producing a melodic line that is as graceful and interesting as it is possible to make it without the aid of durational variety. It is not always easy to achieve a nicely proportioned line within our skeletal limitations of length, range, and rhythm. The essential character of satisfactory melodic curvature can be maintained, however. The following considerations will help you gain grace and interest in your models.

Contour

The first consideration is the overall contour of the model. Three basic types are possible:

1. The type in which all the tones except the first and last lie *below* the pitch level of the tonic (Ex. 3.31a)
2. The type in which all the tones except the first and last lie *above* the pitch level of the tonic (Ex. 3.31b)
3. The type which includes tones both below *and* above the tonic (Ex. 3.31c)

3.31

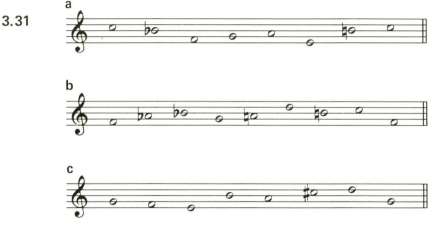

The third type is generally to be preferred. The first lacks the expressive focus of an upper climax tone. The second is greatly to be preferred over the first, since it gains an upper climax even though sacrificing a lower one to balance it. Although the first is not forbidden, it is profitable to bear in mind that an upper climax, for both physical and psychological reasons, produces greater tension than a lower one. It thus not only imparts greater focus to the line, but at the same time renders the ultimate tonic a more convincing haven of rest. The third type not only achieves an upper climax but balances it with a lower one. This adds a tension of polarity in relation to the tonal center—like stretching and releasing an elastic band—which finds satisfying release in the last tone. In Example 3.31b and c, note that the upper climaxes occur nearer to the end than to the beginning. This is not an immutable principle and can sometimes be effectively disregarded. But usually the buildup of tension requires more time than the release.

Look again at all three of the models in Example 3.31, which demonstrate another very important principle governing the use of climax tones: no climax tone should ever be repeated. Far from adding emphasis in these small surroundings, such repetition is merely anticlimactic (Ex. 3.32).

3.32

rep.

Proportion

The second consideration in producing a graceful and interesting model is the proportion between its parts, its length, and its range—its overall melodic gesture. With so few notes available, both horizontally and vertically, it is generally better not to "give it all away" at once. Therefore, any group of notes threatening to usurp too great a portion of the available length or range must be either carefully controlled or avoided altogether. There are three groups in this category:

> 1. Too many notes moving in the same direction (Ex. 3.33). Change direction after four at the most. Remember to avoid triads!

3.33

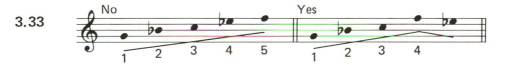

> 2. Any skip larger than a perfect fifth. Such a skip must be avoided. Even the skip of a fifth (Ex. 3.34) uses up half the available range. This skip may be followed by *one step only* in the same direction, after which the direction must change. Similarly, it may be preceded by one step in the same direction. P5 may in fact be preceded *and* followed by a step in the same direction, though a strong cadence may be difficult to achieve if these are the last four tones of a model.

3.34

> 3. Two adjacent skips in the same direction (Ex. 3.35). Any such pair of skips would use up almost the whole range even if it did not outline a triad (already prohibited).

3.35

etc.

WRITING PERFECT MODELS

You now have all the factual information you need to write perfect models.* If you find the process somewhat difficult in the beginning, it is partly for the simple reason that there are so many things to remember. As you begin, the quickest way to achieve success is to choose the first note and write it down. Then write down every note that could possibly follow it and choose one. Repeat the process in arriving at each tone until the model has regained the tonic. In this way you are not likely to deny yourself possibilities which are freely permissible within the framework of the rules. In some cases there will be more possibilities than in others. Very soon you will begin to perceive these possibilities and make the choices almost instinctively—using the checklist only after the model is finished.

With a few such efforts the rules will shed their tyranny and you will begin to exercise more and more control over linear contours and tonal centers.

> Before going on, practice writing models until your work is free of any but the most occasional error.

A time will come when you feel that all your models are very much alike. When that time arrives, look over Example 3.36. It shows every permissible combination of three notes with which a model can begin. Try making models with a few of the combinations you have not yet used.

 3.36

*In Appendix 1 you will find a numbered checklist of rules for quick reference as you begin work. Use it strictly as such, not as a substitute for rereading the text whenever some aspect of the work is unclear to you. (Each item in the checklist carries a page reference to the corresponding discussion in the text.) Occasionally, in this and subsequent chapters, these rules will be referred to by number.

As soon as you feel that you are fully in command of the more mechanical aspects of the technique, you will be free to experiment with all sorts of things: contours, placement of climax tones, exploitation of both minimal and maximal pitch range, intervalic variety, properly handled tone repetitions, minimal and maximal use of properly handled augmented and diminished intervals, minimum and maximum length (including more than a dozen tones), etc. Your most interesting and fruitful experiments, however, will be concerned with controlling the strength or weakness of the tonal center, to which all the other experiments are related and can be contributory. This concern merits some detailed attention.

Emphasizing the Tonic

This discipline recognizes your probable orientation toward tonality, though it seeks to lead your ear and your writing hand toward broader and more nearly current usages. The work is therefore designed to make it almost impossible for you to adhere strictly to all the stylistic tenets of tonality. Nevertheless, it is possible to produce models, such as the five in Example 3.37, in which certain obvious factors unequivocally emphasize a strictly tonal tonic:

1. Exclusive use of the tones of one of the four tonal scales—the major scale and the ascending, descending, and harmonic minor scales
2. Strategic placement of the tonally functional tones—tonic, dominant, subdominant, and lower leading tone—at the end for greatest strength, at the beginning for somewhat less strength, and in the departure for minimum effect

3.37

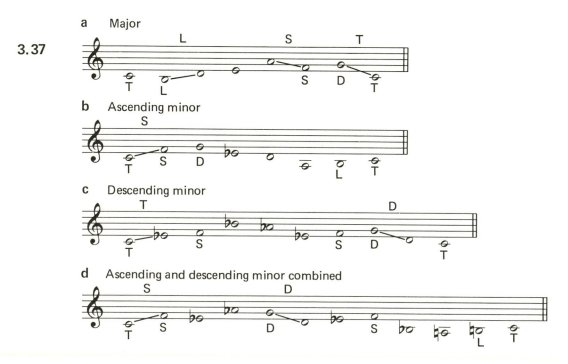

a   Major

b   Ascending minor

c   Descending minor

d   Ascending and descending minor combined

e Harmonic minor

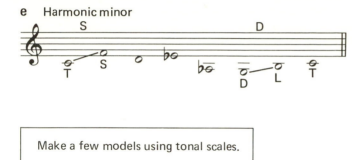

Make a few models using tonal scales.

Weakening the Tonic

An unobtrusive step toward weakening the tonic would be to dilute the tonal scales while still retaining the strategic placement of functional tones. Dilution of the scales can be brought about only by the use of the augmented unison and/or the augmented or diminished octave. The dissolving effect of these intervals will be determined not only by their number, but also by their location and whether or not any of the functional tones are involved. It is difficult to measure the degree of dilution precisely, but the six models in Example 3.38 retain strategic functional placement and are ordered approximately according to their degree of scale dilution:

1. In 3.38a—one d8
2. In 3.38b—one A1 involving leading tone
3. In 3.38c—two A1's, one involving a functional tone
4. In 3.38d—one d8, two A1's, each of the three involving functional tones, including the tonic. Any tonic, of course, has two leading-tone satellites—one a half-step above it, the other a half-step below it. When either is heard close to the tonic, the ear clearly perceives the relationship. When the time lapse between the two is great, the relationship is not so obvious. The leading tone may even be more intimately related to some other tone or group of tones, in which case its functional support of the tonic, while still felt, may be only residual. The E♭ in Example 3.38d is a case in point: its relationship to the following D is obvious—it is even enharmonically spelled. Still, its half-step relationship to E, here inverted to d8 (M7), is unmistakable, in this particular instance reinforced by its position as upper climax.*
5. In 3.38e—three A1's, one d8; all three harmonic functional tones affected, including the tonic. This one uses eleven of the twelve tones, with the result that the scale is fairly well diluted.
6. In 3.38f—four A1's; all three harmonic functional tones affected, including the tonic. Again, there are eleven tones, but the functional tones are less strategically placed than in Example 3.38e (early rather than late).

---

*Such semiobscured relationships are enclosed in parentheses in this and the following examples.

3.38

> Make some models using strategically placed harmonic functional tones with diluted scales. See how many of the twelve tones you can include in a few of them.

In the four models of Example 3.39, the dominant and subdominant, while still usually present, are not strategically placed. The cadence is kept reasonably strong, however, by the use of the upper leading tone:

1. In 3.39a—one A1
2. In 3.39b—two A1's
3. In 3.39c—four A1's, involving two functional tones, but no *dominant.* The chromatic step-progression (under the bracket) is a further, is subtle, tonal ambiguity (see Ex. 3.10).

4. In 3.39d—six A1's; two functional tones affected, including the tonic. Again, the dominant is missing.

3.39

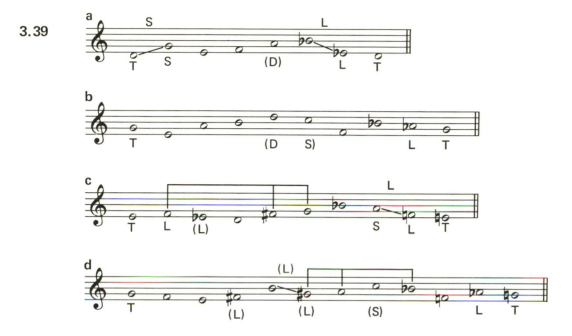

Did you notice the infrequency of functional skips in these four models? The fewer there are, the more ambiguous the tonic. Notice also how often the two members of the A1's have been "squeezed" closer together than previously—there is only one tone between; this is still another factor of ambiguity.

Make a few models in which only the leading tones are strategically placed. Continue to use as many of the twelve tones as possible, and place the A1's, A8's, and d8's as close as possible. Avoid functional skips insofar as feasible.

Further Weakening the Tonic

The three models in Example 3.40 have no genuine strategically placed functional tones other than the tonic at the beginning and the end. The cadences are without direct functional support:

1. In 3.40a—one A1
2. In 3.40b—three A1's, subdominant missing. The stability of the final tonic is further weakened if, as here, that tonic is a member of a squeezed A1 (properly

resolved, of course). Also, notice that the root of the only strong skip (P5) is removed from the tonic by the distance of a tritone—a further tonic disruption.

3. In 3.40c—six A1's, dominant *and* subdominant missing

3.40

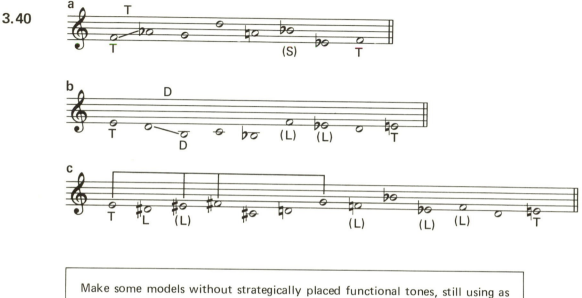

Make some models without strategically placed functional tones, still using as many of the twelve tones as you conveniently can.

While Example 3.41a (one A1) does include two strategically placed functional tones (D and L), the stability of its tonic is all but destroyed by the frequent use of the two exceptions to rule 6 (see Ex. 3.11 and 3.12). The unsettling effect of the diminished and augmented intervals is the justification for rule 6, and the two exceptions are thus useful largely for the departure, where an unsettled quality is desirable. The second exception is here used precisely for its comparatively mild cadential ambiguity but, coupled as it is with the first exception, the result is a considerable degree of instability.

3.41

Example 3.41b (one A1) is the intervalic inversion of Example 3.41a. Its slight decrease in stability can be attributed to the fact that the tonic is no longer the root of the first skip.

> Try a few models with a generous sprinkling of these two exceptions to rule 6.

All the models illustrated up to this point conform strictly to the rules embodied in the chapter. One of the aims of these rules is the establishment and confirmation of the tonic. It must be evident at this point that the rules can accommodate this aim within a very wide range between stability and instability.

Threatening the Tonic

Some instructors and students will wish to explore the "atonal" possibilities beyond the limits thus far illustrated. The remaining examples can facilitate this purpose by means of their more permissive application of one of the rules which are designed to promote stability of the tonal center.

The models in Example 3.42a and b permit the *cadential* use of the formulation shown as the first of the exceptions to rule 6 (see Ex. 3.11):

1. In 3.42a—three A1's, one involving a functional tone. T, D, S, and L are all present as interval roots. The tonic is quite strong in spite of the cadential proximity of the tritone F-B. Much of that stability derives from the presence during the departure of the functional tones as roots of interval skips.
2. The tonic in Example 3.42b (one A1) is immeasurably less stable than in (a). The tritone F-B is aided in its destructive work by the elimination of genuinely functional tones in the departure. The subdominant interval root (enharmonic) loses all functional force through its leading-tone relationship to the B, which is itself in an A4 (very unstable) relationship to the tonic.

3.42

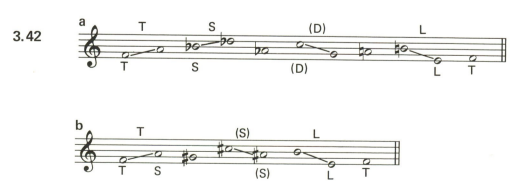

3. and 4. The next two models (Ex. 3.42c and d) use the same unstable three-tone cadential form we saw in Example 3.42a and b, plus the same scarcity of strategically placed functional tones. (d) is the intervalic inversion of (c). The tonal center, not strong in either, is somewhat stronger in (c) than in (d) because the G is more firmly established by the first two tones and because of the leading-tone root of the last skip. In (c), there are three A1's, with the subdominant missing. In (d), also with three A1's, the dominant is missing.

3.42

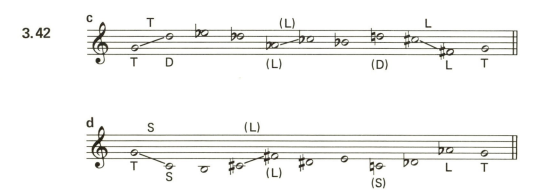

5. and 6. The remarks about Example 3.42c and d are applicable also to (e) and (f), except that the tonics are still more unstable, because of their weaker delineation at the beginning. In both these models, there are three A1's, and in both, D and S are enharmonically present but nonfunctional.

3.42

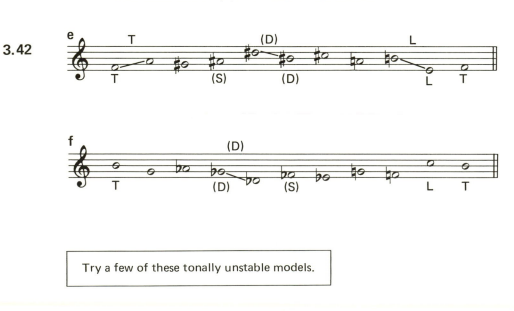

Try a few of these tonally unstable models.

Now turn back to Exercise 3.38f. Play it for yourself, omitting the first note. What do you find? That the F♯, if a convincing tonic at all, is at best considerably short of unequivocal.

Play it again, leaving off the first *and* last notes. The A is also an acceptable tonic—more so than the F♯. The reasons are that it is approached by a stronger interval skip (P4 as against m3) *and* repeats a previous A.

Now play it once again, omitting the first note and the last two. The E is no less viable as a tonic than was the F♯. Like the A, it is also a repetition.

Cut off still one more note at the end. The G would function just as well as a tonic, and for the same reasons.

Now play the whole model. The tonic power of the F♯ is reaffirmed. There are two reasons for this: *any* repetition of a tone lends emphasis, and *any* initial sound makes a unique aural impact which is not easily erased. Its repetition at the end tends to "wrap up" the whole structure, however tenuous its tonic power may be rendered by lack of functional support and by various ambiguous formulations.

Repeat the experiment with the models in Examples 3.39 to 3.42. The results will not be uniform, of course, for the models within each example exhibit progressively weaker tonics, and each example uses a new means for weakening them still further.

The next logical step, which we are not going to take at the moment, would be the elimination of tonal centers altogether. It is not a giant step, but it is a far-reaching one.

You now have achieved a fair degree of technical proficiency as well as some command over the available tonal resources. You will be making models throughout this study. Don't allow yourself to fall into a rut, but think of your models as aids to the exploration of the whole range of tonal stability—from the strongest to the most tenuous.

4 MELODY

I cannot tell you how to make a good melody. If I could, you might find it convenient. But I am not at all sure that the convenience would be salutary, for in the past at least, melody has been the one element of music which most freely accommodated the play of creative individuality. Literally millions of melodies have been written. If even two of them are identical, then the identity is surely the result of accident (barring the time-honored sport of quotation). The same cannot be said of vertical tonal structure (harmony), which composers of the eighteenth century, for example, treated with a considerable degree of uniformity, a uniformity which has persisted in some quarters well into the second half of the twentieth century. Nor has rhythm always been distinguished by notable expressive exploitation, since a certain tyranny of the beat and the bar line are apparently all but inescapable. Until recently the deployment of timbres and textures as primary structural determinants has been largely an inadvertent rather than a conscious manifestation of high art.

While vertical relationships have been limited by what may be termed almost a science of harmony, and while rhythm has suffered from stunted development, melody has brooked no such internal restrictions. To be sure, melody, harmony, rhythm, texture, and timbre must usually be mutually accommodating. And, particularly during the eighteenth and nineteenth centuries, melody had to adapt itself to the dictates of beat, bar, and chord progression. Nonetheless, it has persisted in its preeminence as the most evocative and memorable aspect of music. Could the reason for this possibly be that melody has luckily escaped the tyranny of the rules that have cramped harmony and rhythm? Quite conceivably!

You have already read that the rules in this book are intended to be more a record of cumulative experience than a set of restrictions. Nowhere is that fact more pertinent than in this chapter. I cannot offer you the comfort of a set of rules governing melody making, but I can and will show you some of the principles and techniques that have been useful to composers in the achievement of succinct and compelling melodic utterance. Not all techniques are employed in all melodies, but few melodies entirely escape the influence of these principles. We will examine them one by one in order of convenience rather than of importance—for there really is no perceptible order of importance, so freely are their powers mingled.

Allow me a word on the matter of inspiration. Laymen and novices often assume that melody is above all a gift from heaven—subject neither to conscious effort nor to technical skills. If you entertain a vestige of that superstition, get rid of it at the earliest possible moment. Inspiration is neither more nor less than a capacity for total involvement, usually by the route of hard and persistent cultivation. Technique without imagination is, of course, sterile. But imagination without technique is even worse. If you doubt this, get hold of the published Beethoven sketchbooks and follow the evolution of some of his more "inspired" musical ideas. Inspiration for him consisted in a dogged pursuit of a concept. Or listen to Tchaikovsky: "Madam, for years I have sat down at my writing desk at nine o'clock every morning. The Muses have damned well learned to keep that appointment!"

SHAPE

The term *shape* as used here refers to the manner in which the available pitch range is utilized. That range may be wide or narrow, or it may fall anywhere between these extremes. It might be determined by any of a number of factors—expressive purpose, the medium for which the melody is written, the texture of which the melody is a part, the length of the melody, or even the speed with which it moves. But whatever the extent of that range, the "space" within it must be used purposefully and decisively. More than anything else, this means care in choosing and placing the outer extremes—the highest and lowest tones—of each melodic contour or gesture. It is particularly important in respect to the climaxes, the upper and lower extremities of the melody as a whole. We will call these upper and lower climax tones, together with the first and last tones, the *primary shape tones.* They define the overall shape of the melody.

The overall shape of the Béla Bartók melody in Example 4.1* consists of a gentle, if not quite direct, rise from the G♯ in the first bar to the D♯ in bar 8, followed by a long *denouement* (recession) down to the final D♯ (E♭) in bar 13, two octaves below the upper climax. Note that the upper climax occurs shortly after midpoint. In Example 4.2, these primary shape tones are identified by the symbol □ and by the bracket above the staff.

Within this overall shape there are other, less sweeping, gestures, shown in Example 4.2 by the symbol △ and by the brackets below the staff. *Secondary shape tones* is the term we will apply to the tones occupying the contoural extremities of these less sweeping gestures.

Some of these gestures are further divided into still smaller ones, brought about by each change in the direction of the line. These we will call *tertiary shape tones* and will identify by the symbol ▲ and by the connecting dashes in Example 4.2, which is a diagram intended to make graphically clear what happens in this melody in regard to shape. Compare it minutely with the complete melody (Ex. 4.1).

---

*Example 4.1 is notated in the C clef, which is used for viola parts. Also called the viola clef or the alto clef, it places middle C on the third line of the staff. If you do not yet read this clef easily, you should learn to do so now, as familiarity with it is part of musical literacy. As a first step, copy the melody of Example 4.1 in the treble clef.

from Béla Bartók, *String Quartet No. 6*

4.1

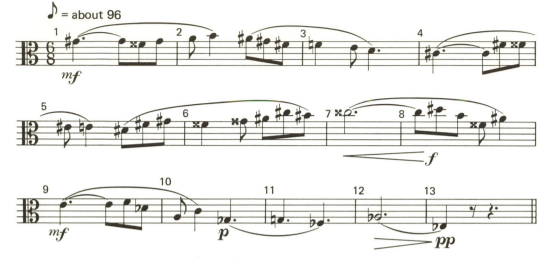

4.2

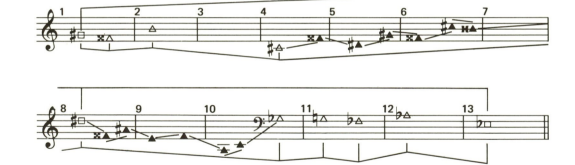

What Example 4.2 proves, perhaps, is that while a straight line may be the shortest distance between two points, it is not necessarily the most interesting nor the most meaningful. Play Example 4.1 and follow it immediately with Example 4.3, which exploits the same overall shape as Bartók's melody, but reduces it to absurdity by substituting the most arid mechanical means for Bartók's graceful, undulating melodic contours.

4.3

Liken the primary shape tones, if you will, to the skeleton of the body, the secondary tones to the flesh, and the tertiary tones to the heart, which endows the whole with its lifeblood. Is the point clear? The interplay of rhythm, pitch, length, range, and shape within and among the various gestures is a major factor in the expressive vitality of a melody. If these gestures are eradicated or simplified to mechanical contrivance, the point of the whole melody is lost and the overall shape becomes nothing more than an empty shell.

STRESSED TONES

Quite instinctively, the ear attributes a greater importance to the primary shape tones of a melody than it does to the surrounding, or intervening, ones. The former are unconsciously remembered as turning points or even hard-earned goals. The high D♯ in Example 4.1, for instance, seems to *snap* the melody off and hurl it in another direction. The same is true, but perhaps to a lesser degree, of the secondary and tertiary shape tones as well. Most of these tones in fact tend to receive a certain stress which creates a sort of hierarchy among all the tones of a melody.

There are many ways in which tones may be stressed:

1. By contour, as described on pages 41-43
2. By sheer duration in relation to the surrounding tones—in Example 4.1, for instance, the first G♯, the high C✗, the last five tones, etc.
3. By half-step resolution of a leading tone, especially if that leading tone is also stressed—the A♯ in bar 2, C♯ in bar 4, F✗ in bar 6 (two half-step relationships), D♯ in bar 8, etc.
4. By being the second or goal tone of a large skip—F♯ in bar 4, A♯ in bar 8, E in bar 9, etc.
5. By being the first or last tone of a phrase or motive (to be defined later in the chapter), or even of a whole melody—G♯ in bar 1 and D in bar 3 (phrase), E in bar 9 and C in bar 10 (motive)
6. By repetition—G♯ and G♯ in bar 1 (not a particularly good example. Why?)
7. By membership in a simple and obvious chord structure—D♯ in bar 5; F✗, A♯, and C♯ in bar 6
8. By resolution of tension—in Example 4.1 the only good illustration is the high D♯. In an unaccompanied melody there are no *diads* (vertical intervals) to produce intervalic tension. Here one feels tension in the C✗ because a D♯ dominant seventh chord has just been outlined. F in bar 9 qualifies to a degree because of the tritone skip just before it.
9. By dynamic emphasis—D♯ in bar 8 and E♭ in bar 13
10. By metric accent (falling on the strong part of several successive measures). There are no genuine metric stresses in the Bartók melody, despite a certain—if inconsistent—periodicity stemming from the durational stresses at bars 1, 4, and 7. Note also the unresolved conflict between the 6/8 barring and the almost consistent 9/8 pulse organization.

4.4

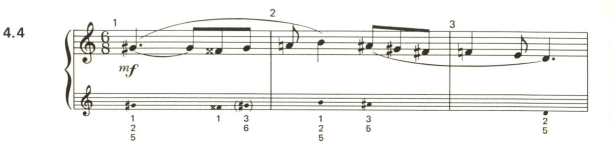

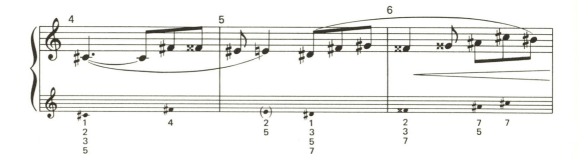

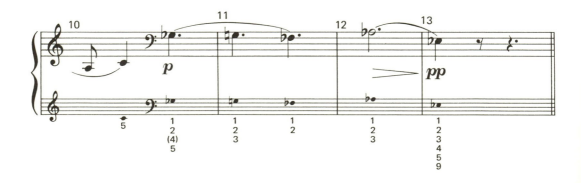

Example 4.4 shows Bartók's melody with the various stressed tones given on a second staff. Each stressed tone is numbered to show which of the ten means previously discussed produces, or produce, the stress. Obviously, a tone may be stressed simultaneously by more than one means. As the upper climax, the D♯ in bar 8, for instance, quite logically carries more stress—six means—than any other tone except the final E♭ (D♯). The only other tones with more than three stresses, C♯ in bar 4 and D♯ in bar 5, are also contourally and tonally important ones.

However, if you compare Examples 4.2 and 4.4, you will see that the stressed tones and the tones which define the shapes within the melody do not necessarily coincide. The *shape* tones, especially the tertiary ones, often have other functions than carrying the action forward from one salient point to the next: aesthetic seductiveness, for instance, rather than structural security. Another of these functions, a very important one, is tonal organization.

TONAL ORGANIZATION

A melody can—and most melodies do—establish some sort of hierarchy among the tones. This principle has not been completely invalidated by the "demise" of tonality. The establishment of tonal centers and the control of their strength were discussed in Chapter 3. Since for the present your melodies will be pegged to the tonally coherent models you have already learned to write, it is reasonably safe to predict that these melodies will be tonally coherent. Nevertheless, since the tones of your model will be the stress tones in your melodies, you will soon see that you can stress some tones more than others, and thereby possibly temper the obviousness of the tonal center.

Let us examine first the obvious factors in Bartók's tonal scheme. The tonic is clearly G♯, with G♯, D♯ (dominant), and C♯ (subdominant) prominent among the secondary tones (see Ex. 4.2). Also among the secondary shape tones are two leading tones supporting the G♯ (F𝗑 in bar 1 and G in bar 11). D♯ also has the support of two leading tones (C𝗑 in bar 7 and F♭ in bar 11).*

Another strong factor supporting the tonic in this melody is the outlining, by stress and skip, of the dominant seventh chord on D♯ (D♯ in bar 5 with F𝗑, A♯, and C♯ in bar 6). Another is the drop from tonic to dominant outlined by the last two notes.

The amount of support given to the tonic by these functionally related tones could easily render the whole thing overobvious. But Bartók has taken counter steps. He has used none of the scales which would have spelled out the tonic unmistakably. Instead, he presents a variety of three-note groups comprising equal intervals (see Ex. 3.10 and reread the comments about it). These groups amount to a string of ambiguities which balance the strength of tonic support:

1. Consecutive half-steps (Ex. 4.5a)
2. Three-note groups covering an M2 span as in (1), but reordered (Ex. 4.5b)
3. Contiguous major thirds, creating a dichotomy of roots (Ex. 4.5c)
4. Groups comprising two m3's and a tritone (Ex. 4.5d)

*To be statistical for a moment: of the 62 stresses marked in Example 4.4, 41 are concentrated on these six tones—28 of these on the tonic, dominant, and subdominant alone. This leaves only 21 stresses for the other six tones combined, one of which, A, receives no stress at all.

4.5

The tritone renders the groups in Example 4.5d perhaps the most ambiguous of all. (Because of its extreme instability and unpredictability, it was once called "the devil in music.") The only certainty about these particular tritones is that none of their normal resolutions would lead to G♯!

I think that if you play and listen to this Bartók melody repeatedly and thoughtfully, you will come to sense how the tonal strengths are balanced by the ambiguities. But these two factors also create a powerful conflict—the solid tonal elements always trying to repair the "damage" done them by the ambiguities, even while the ambiguities are continually flying in the face of the established tonal foundations. May you develop some of Bartók's skill!

PHRASE

Few indeed are the melodies that run on from beginning to end without letup. Of course, from time to time it might be fun for the composer to see just how long he can suspend the listener or entice him to hold his breath. But sooner or later, like dancers, both performer and listener must land on the floor with both feet and get a good breath of air. The phrase allows this to happen. The singer needs the pause not only to replace expended air, but also for the support of vocal tone production. In empathy, the listener succumbs to these physical requirements so completely that almost inadvertently they emerge as psychological expectations as well. Thus, even when music is written for instruments which have no breath requirements, such as the piano or violin, phrase divisions are usually present.

In Example 4.6, the brackets above the staff indicate the phrase structure of the Bartók melody. Notice the intimate relationship between the phrases and the primary and secondary shape tones which, as you have seen, are in *this* instance tonally functional as well. This intimate relationship, while common in the music of earlier centuries, has become less so with the general disintegration of structural tonality in the late nineteenth and early twentieth centuries. Notice also the overlap between the second and third phrases, which surely contributes to the forward compulsion.

4.6

In this melody, only two of the four phrases are equal in length (3, 4⅓, 3½, and 3 bars respectively). This creates a subtle tension. For example, by the time you have heard the A♯ in the second phrase, you might very well expect a pause on that note, since up to that point the second phrase has been rhythmically an exact repetition of the first. But no—you must hold your breath through nearly two more bars. Even then, because of the overlap, you get only a quick "catch" breath. Do you sense the exhaustion as the line droops in the third phrase, then slows down and retreats to extinction in the fourth? If it were possible to clearly define what differentiates good music from bad, then surely high on the list would be the skill with which the composer makes each phrase not only lead to, but demand, the next.

MOTIVE

The motive is the smallest melodic unit capable of conveying a relatively independent statement, however incomplete that statement may be. The elements discussed up to now —shape, stress, tonal organization, and phrase—important as they are, hardly touch on the musical character or expressive quality of the melody. Indeed, these elements could almost be interchangeable among several different melodies of wildly divergent character. We have examined them without reference to tempo, articulation, dynamics, or the relative "smoothness" or "jaggedness" of either pitch or rhythm. These latter elements are almost invariably set forth by the first few scraps of sound to reach the ear, and the first motive of the Bartók melody (Ex. 4.7) is no exception.

4.7

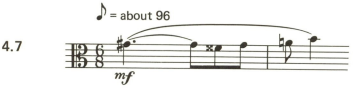

We get a good deal of information from this bar and a half:

    Tempo—slow, hardly more than a pulse every other second
    Articulation—slurred, legato
    Dynamics—*mf*; neither aggressive nor recessive, but "easy"
    Pitch—smooth; conjunct motion exclusively
    Rhythm—smooth again; preponderance of equal durations
    Tonal character—ambiguous
    Contour—gentle rise (questioning?)

So you see the motive is very important. It is, so to speak, the thesis of the whole melody, and the composer's skill in developing that thesis is crucial. If he should wander too far away from the characteristics of the motive, especially in an illogical fashion, his melody may very well sound scatterbrained. On the other hand, overslavish repetitions of these characteristics will most certainly be dull and inconsequential. The motive is the means by which the composer figuratively takes the listener by the hand and leads him through the ramifications of his melodic discourse toward whatever point he wishes to make clear.

Look at Example 4.6 again and let us see how Bartók manages this in the melody we have been examining. The brackets *below* the staff indicate the motives. As in most melodies, more than one motive is used; in this case, there are two. Like all motives, each of these has three distinguishing aspects—interval content, contour, and rhythm. The concentrated impact of this melody is a result at least in part of the similarity between the two motives:

    Interval content—identical (M2 and m2)
    Contour—motive 1: upward, one change of direction
            motive 2: downward

Rhythm—motive 1: ♩. ♫♩ ♪♩

motive 2: ♫♩ ♪♩.

If the motive is the smallest relatively independent melodic unit, the phrase is usually the smallest reasonably complete unit within which the motive can change, develop, or coexist with one or more other motives. I hope you will note the following compositional niceties of phrase-motive relationship in Example 4.6:

1. Phrases 1 and 2 use both motives in the same order. Phrase 3 uses only motive 1, phrase 4 only motive 2. Note the stretching of the second phrase by repetition of motive 2, altered, and pivoting on the A♯ in bar 6.

2. In bars 7 and 8, the overlap of motives corresponds to the overlap of phrases.

3. As the chief factor employed to identify each motive, rhythm alone remains constant except for the two augmentations in bars 7 and 10. The first augmentation is for the purpose of strategically placed suspense, while the second accomplishes an appropriate fade-out. The final tone of motive 2 is twice omitted.*

4. While rhythm remains almost changeless, intervalic content changes drastically with each appearance of the motives, each time enhancing interest by the replacement of steps with skips. Note especially the preponderance of skips in motive 1 as employed in the third phrase. By this means, even though post-climactic intensity recedes, interest is by no means allowed to flag—quite the contrary! Here is a breakdown of the number of skips in each successive appearance:

	Motive 1	Motive 2
First appearance	0	0
Second appearance	1	1
Third appearance	3	1
Fourth appearance	3	3

5. The contour of each motive changes also, in close keeping with the expressive intent in each instance. These changes are drastic. Not only does the general *directional thrust* of each motive show purposeful changes, but the *number* of directional changes within succeeding appearances of each motive is revealing:

	Motive 1	Motive 2
First appearance	1	0
Second appearance	1	2
Third appearance	2	2
Fourth appearance	2	3

*The fact that in this melody rhythm remains a constant factor while the other motivic ingredients develop is not necessarily typical. But motivic identity is almost invariably essential to melodic coherence, and Bartók has here merely used the most readily memorable of the three ingredients to that end. Either of the others might serve as well, but perhaps with a bit more difficulty.

Statistics do not make music, of course, but it would be foolish to overlook this cumulative intervallic and contoural growth as powerful ingredients in Bartók's capacity to maintain our interest and seduce us into full involvement in his melody.

BINDING FORCES

A number of additional devices have been employed by composers either to bind the parts of a melody into a coherent whole, to enhance the urgency of its forward motion, to create still another source of subtle tension, or to relate its formal divisions:

1. The *step-progression* is exactly what the term implies—a series of tones, touched on in the course of a melody, which form a stepwise progression, often interrupted by intervening tones but sometimes including contiguous tones, usually headed toward and thus emphasizing an important tonal or formal goal. Step-progressions are present in all the melodies illustrated in this chapter, and some of them will be pointed out to you.
2. The *holding tone* is like the step-progression in function, but instead of moving stepwise from one tone to the next it is stationary—returning repeatedly to a single tone. It is often merely a temporary cessation of motion in a longer step-progression.
3. The *chord-outline progression* is another variant of the step-progression. It emphasizes, with intervening tones, the members of a simple triad or seventh chord.
4. A *cell* is a tiny rhythmic or melodic unit consisting of two or three tones. It hardly has the significance of a motive, but it can sometimes serve as a binding force if it is emphasized by its placement.
5. The *cadence formula* is a short motive or cell serving consistently to identify the ends of several phrases. It is usually not used elsewhere in the melody.
6. The *phrase head* is a short motive or cell used to call attention to the beginnings of phrases. Like the cadence formula, it is seldom used elsewhere in the melody.

The Bartók Melody Again

Example 4.8, the Bartók melody with which you are now so familiar, shows several step-progressions used in a rather delightfully subtle manner. They are numbered for you in the example. Some of these step-progressions are very important to the structure—notably (1), which begins on the opening G♯ and climbs to the D♯ climax, and the wedgelike pair—(4a and 6)—pointing up the final skip from tonic to dominant. The others are less obvious in effect. (4), the one initiated by the C♯ in bar 4 and rising through D♯ to E and F in bar 9, is here joined, because of the octave break, by a dotted line to the G♭ in bar 10 and proceeds presumably through G to the last A♭. This is interesting because, without this tenuous connection, the middle of bar 10 would be the only phrase break or motive connection not overridden by a binding step-progression. Players often make this distinction in their performance.

4.8

Note that the tones of the step-progressions in this melody occur at rather un-predictable time intervals. This lends to the whole an additional dimension of subtlety and tension. In bar 9, particularly, the E and the D♭ pick up progressions apparently long since abandoned, effectively relating the second and third acts of the mini-drama!

Other binding forces in the Bartók melody are the gently felt chord-outline progression D♯, F✕, A♯, and C♯ in bars 5 and 6 (already referred to on page 43, list item 8), and a two-tone cell: G♯-F✕ in bar 1, B-A♯ in bar 2, C♯-B♯ in bar 6, and finally its inversion C✕-D♯ in bars 7 and 8 to cap the climax. This little sequence, riding the crest of the melodic contours, contributes to the urgency of the rise to the climax.

A Handel Melody

The melody in Example 4.9, from a flute sonata by George Frederick Handel, illustrates several of the binding forces, including three holding tones, which appear under the brackets marked (2). The repeated C in bar 2 is placed in a position of tension with D and F♯; the A in bar 3 is in a similar relationship to B and D♯. This prolongs the tension and adds emphasis to their resolutions in the second half of beat 3 in bar 2 and the first beat of bar 4, respectively. Both these holding tones form part of larger step-progressions.

from G. F. Handel, *Flute Sonata,* Op. 1, No. 1b

4.9

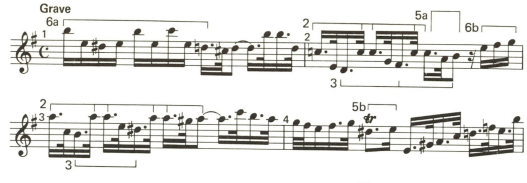

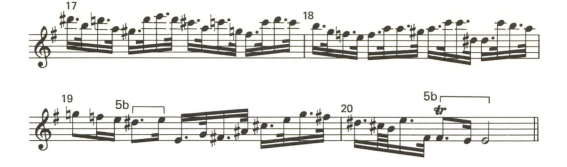

The third holding tone performs somewhat differently. The low F♯ in bar 7 is the terminus of a long step-progression which began on the very first note of the piece. It is not restruck until nearly a bar later, and by this time the composer is ready to reveal that low F♯ as the functional dominant of B, on which the following phrase will cadence. This B cadence secures the dominant of the piece at the approximate halfway point, and is second in importance only to the final cadence on the tonic.

There are two chord-outline progressions—(3)—both, in this case, employed in conjunction with holding tones. Both outline simple triads: in bar 2, one in B minor (B, D, F♯), and in bar 3, in B major (B, D♯, F♯). The F♯ is missing in the second, but the members of the chord which are functional in the E minor tonic (D and L) are there. Since B is the dominant, these chord-outline progressions not only promote melodic cohesion, but serve a harmonic function as well.

Two cadence formulas also appear in Example 4.9, and (5b) identifies the three important full cadences—those on the dominant (bar 11), the tonic (bar 20), and the relative major (bar 6). (The relative major, because it embraced the same tones as its relative minor, was considered an important tonal relationship just so long as scales were an identifiable structural factor.) The first two notes of (5b) are also used at the points of phrase elision (bars 4 and 19).

The secondary cadences (those on less important tonal levels) are identified by (5a) in bars 2, 8, and 13. There is only one cadence, in bar 16, where neither formula is used.

Two different phrase heads are used in the Handel, each in a different way. The first—(6a)—is used only at the beginnings of the two larger sections of the piece—both times in the tonic key (bars 1 and 12). It thus lends melodic emphasis to very important tonal and formal spots. (6b), an upbeat of three sixteenth-notes, introduces all the remaining phrases except in the two places where there are elisions (bars 4 and 19).

By these two means (cadence formula and phrase head), Handel has not only set off each phrase very clearly, but he has at the same time related each phrase to all the others in such a way as to establish a hierarchy among them which serves his formal and expressive purposes most admirably.

The step-progression is so copiously employed in this melody as to seem perhaps overdone. I will point out only three instances of it in order to illustrate how Handel has turned it to his purpose:

1. E and D (bar 1) to C and B (bar 2). B restruck (bar 3), then not again (in the same octave) until bar 7, where it joins another already in progress.

2. B, C, and B (bar 1); A (bar 3); G, F♯, E, and D♮ (bar 4); C♯ (bar 5) to B (bar 7). From here step-progressions (1) and (2) move on together through A, G♯, and G♮ to the low F♯ (bar 7), which in turn becomes the third holding tone (page 50).

3. Low D (bar 2); E (bar 4); F♯ in (bars 7 and 8); E (bar 12); D (bar 13); E and F♯ (bar 19); F♯ and E (bar 20). This one runs through the whole melody and its tones are very widely spaced. Its slow pace and continuous presence furnish a broad backdrop against which the various speeds and lengths of the many others stand in sharp contrast and produce a subtle underlying tension. This is a fairly common device, and we will encounter it again in the melody by Elliott Carter.

> There are many more step-progressions in Example 4.9. In most cases there are several running along simultaneously. Search them out.

A Webern Melody

The melody in Example 4.10, from a song by Anton Webern, illustrates a more subtle, if diluted, use of the phrase head and the cadence formula. The phrase head (6) is particularly interesting here because of the amount of rhythmic variation to which it is subjected without losing its identity:

Statement (bar 1)
Repetition (bar 3)
Augmentation (bar 6 [7])
Diminution (bar 8)
First note omitted (bar 12)
First note partially restored (bar 14)
First note fully restored (bar 16)
Augmentation with two intervening notes (bar 18)

It is, of course, subjected to an equal amount of pitch variation, recurring only once on the original pitches. Amid all this rhythmic and pitch variation, however, one rhythmic factor allows this phrase head to perform its function—it never loses the quality of an upbeat, though it is not always an upbeat to the first beat of a bar.

One of the melodic subtleties which contribute to this melody's persuasive charm is the frequency with which the phrase head verges on loss of identity without actually losing it—the last three tones in bars 2 and 5, for example, are so similar to the phrase head that if the phrases were not set apart by rests at this point, the phrase head might lose some of its identifying power in later elided phrases.

Search out other such instances of subtle phrase head treatment in Example 4.10.

from Anton Webern, *Fünf Lieder,* Op. 4

4.10

The cadence formula does not undergo nearly as much rhythmic variation as does the phrase head. It consists usually of two eighths followed by a rest. Pitch variation runs rampant, however, and only once does the cadence formula repeat itself on a previously heard pitch level. It is interesting that these are the last two appearances. Perhaps this is Webern's method of conveying a sense of finality in the midst of a tonal language which, considering the date of composition (1909), is not given to tonal conclusiveness. The cadence formula is perhaps more diluted by use in the body of the phrases than is the phrase head. The delightful ambiguity here is that the listener is never quite sure which is being subjected to dilution!

Step-progressions are employed in the Webern melody, but not nearly as obviously as in the Handel. One of them is bracketed below the staff in the first phrase. Notice the long, slow one which begins with the very first C (repeated in bar 5), moves to C♯ at the end of the third phrase in bar 8, and finishes off the fourth phrase with the D in bar 10. This also concludes the first half of the piece.

> Search out other step-progressions in Example 4.10.

A Bach Melody

Any good melody exhibits many facets, any one of which could rivet our interest, and Example 4.11, from J. S. Bach's English Suite No. 5, is no exception. It is included here to show the artful way in which the composer has used three tiny and simple rhythmic cells to define his form and achieve his artistic purpose. The three cells, each occupying one beat, are:

Three further rhythmic gestures appear cadentially or as connecting links, but hardly figure in the rhythmic development.

The melody is easily divisible into two-bar units. Table 4.1 shows graphically how the cells are placed, or ordered, within each of those units. If a cell is itself altered, the alteration is described in parentheses. Any beat in which none of the cells appears is indicated by a zero.

Study the outline carefully, always playing the melody, or pertinent part thereof, in order to hear and understand the musical effect of what you are observing. Note the following points:

1. The original order of the cells is employed only four times, always leading to a cadence on a functional tone (the relative major served as such in Bach's time) and/or setting off one of the principal sections.

from J. S. Bach, *English Suite No. 5,* Sarabande

4.11

Table 4.1

Unit Number	Bars	Cell Order and Variation	Comments
1	1-2	1,2,2 / 3,0,0	original order
2	3-4	1,2,2 / 3,0,0	original order
3	5-6	1,2,0 / 1,2,3	
4	7-8	3,2,2 / 3,0,0	nearly original order
End of first section—dominant			
5	9-10	3,2,2 / 3,0,0	repeat order of unit 4, which omits cell 1
6	11-12	3,2,2 / 3,0,0	
7	13-14	1,2,3(snap) / 1(R)[1],1,1(R in D[2])	maximum cell variation
8	15-16	1,2,2 / 3,0,0	original order
End of second section—subdominant			
9	17-18	3,1(R),0 / 1,1(R),0	
10	19-20	3,1(R),0 / 1,1(R),0	
11	21-22	3,2,2 / 1(R),1,2	
12	23-24	1,2,2 / 3,0,0	original order
End of third section and of piece—tonic			

[1] R—retrograde (backwards)

[2] D—diminished (note values reduced)

2. The construction of each section, in terms of cell order, is the same—two identical units, one unit with contrasting cell order, and one unit in the original order (except the nearly original order in the first section). This provides each section with a miniform consisting of a beginning (units 1 and 2 in section 1), a departure (unit 3), and an end (unit 4 in section 1).

3. The melody as a whole exhibits rhythmically a similar beginning (the original order in the tonic—unit 1), departure (units 2 through 11, climaxing in units 7 through 10, where the cells themselves are subjected to variation as well as re-ordering), and a return home of the end (unit 12, which restores the original order in the tonic).

4. The first two units of each succeeding section borrow and exploit something from the previous section. Thus units 5 and 6 borrow and exploit the nearly original order with which unit 4 closed off section 1. Units 9 and 10 borrow and exploit the cell variation which constituted the departure (unit 7) in section 2. Both continuity and cumulative interest are thus served.

5. Cell 3 occurs in tandem only once (over the bar line between units 3 and 4), employing increased rhythmic activity to cap the step-progression climax in section 1.

6. At the beginning of section 2, that upper step-progression is carried on to the thrice-heard high B, and then tosses the responsibility for continued interest and tension to the rhythmic variations of the cells themselves, and of their order, in unit 7. (Note that unit 6 is an intervalic inversion of unit 5.)

7. The sequence in unit 3 by which the G climax is reached reappears in unit 9. This time there is rhythmic intensification achieved through a reordering of cells and the use of cell 1 retrograde. Furthermore, the sequence is extended through unit 10, again to push toward the climactic A in bar 21.

8. Unit 11, a pure delight, functions as a bridge between the rhythmic departures of units 7, 9, and 10, and the return of the original order (unit 12). It begins by exploiting the nearly original order of unit 4. But instead of the four notes of cell 3 which have been rendered predictable by six earlier 22/3 cell orders (units 1, 2, 4, 5, 6, and 8), we have only the first three (cell 1 retrograde). Cell 1 is immediately restored in the next beat, preparing for the final original cell order.

It is easy enough to tabulate these cells and units. Anyone who can count to 24 can accomplish that. The important thing is to speculate about why Bach used them as he did. *Do so,* using the few hints I have given you.

For example, do you suppose Bach introduced that retrograde of cell 1 way back in bar 14 just in order to be able to fool us in bar 22, where cell 2 in tandem has led us to expect the whole of cell 3 instead of only its first three notes—the retrograde? Or does he, having introduced the retrograde quite capriciously in bar 14, merely seize on its use in bar 22 as a final spur to interest and a convenient bridge back from the rhythmic departures inaugurated in bar 5?

Only a very good piece of music can raise such questions. If the composer had used those three cells in a less logical fashion, or if he had used an arbitrarily large number of different cells, then the framework might have been so broad that how he had used them would not have mattered in the least. The consequence would be indifference on the part of the listener. No artist can tolerate that.

It is most important to understand that in this melody Bach uses his rhythmic cells (see Table 4.2), within each section as well as in the whole piece, as we use the tones in making a model.

Table 4.2

Model	*Bach Melody*
Establishing the tonic	Establishing the order of cells
Departure Exploits a variety of tones, relationships, and resultant tensions.	Departure Exploits variations on the cells and their order, fomenting tensions through new juxtapositions.
Returning to tonic Releases tension through final progression to final tonic.	Returning to original order Releases tension through bridge back to original order.

TWO MELODIES COMPARED

The last melody to be looked at, and the most recently composed, is Example 4.12, from the viola cadenza in Elliott Carter's String Quartet No. 2. Though not as obviously perceptible here, most of the factors discussed in relation to the four previous melodies are just as clearly at work. The example shows what the viola plays from bars 135 to 154 in the printed score. Read only the upper staff in each system. (The lower staves will be discussed later.)

from Elliott Carter, *String Quartet No. 2*

4.12

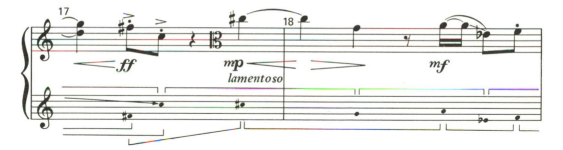

In several manifestations of principle, this melody is comparable to the Bach melody you have just been studying. In the application of these principles it is quite different.

Tonal Organization

The tonal center is far more tenuous in the Carter. Bach establishes his through the use of scales, conventional root sequences, and by sectional cadences on functional tones. In the Carter melody the A is supported by the following:

1. Melodic progressions from G♯ to A—bars 6, 10, and 14
2. Melodic progression from B♭ to A—bars 19 and 20
3. Melodic progression from G to A (not strong in itself)—bars 18 and 20
4. Accented cadence on E (dominant)—bar 12. (This E is immediately preceded by *its* leading tone, F; that F is preceded by G.)
5. Subsequent emphasis on E through ministep-progression G-F-E (same three tones)—bars 15 and 16. (F and G had, up to this point, served as leading tones to rival tonal center, F♯, in bars 3 and 4, 7, and 11—end of rival tonic.)
6. Complementary step-progression to E—C♯ (bar 13), D♯ (bar 14), E (bar 16)
7. Prominent association of E (dominant) with B♭ (leading tone)—bars 8, 16, and 19
8. Eventual resolution of the above tritone—B♭ (bar 19) to A (bar 20)
9. Chord-outline progressions—C♯-E-G-A, root A (bars 19 and 20); F-D-B♭-A♭, root B♭, two leading tones to A (bars 18 and 19)

All accents are rather pointedly placed on the tones discussed above as tonic support, or on the rival tonic, F♯—except B in bar 16 (pitch climax of whole melody), and F♯-C in bar 17 (last gasp of F♯ association).

Carter uses other binding step-progressions in addition to those already mentioned. Here are three of them:

1. B♭ (bars 4 and 8); B (bar 8); C (bar 9); D♭ (bar 12); D (bar 13); D♯ (bar 14); E (bar 16); F♯ (bar 17)
2. E♭ (bar 1); F (bar 5); F♯ (bar 11—end of rival tonic); G (bars 16 and 19); A (bar 20)
3. A (bar 3); A♭, A, B (bar 6); C (bar 11); D (bar 14); E♭, F (bar 18)—here joining chord-outline progression F-D-B♭-A♭

Rhythmic Activity

Instances of the intensification of rhythmic activity for strategic purposes in the Bach melody are, among others, the tandem use of cell 3 (bars 6 and 7), and the adjacent use of cell 3 and cell 1 retrograde (bars 17 and 19).

In the Carter melody, this is done by the subtle introduction and exploitation of shorter note values (here interpreted as the time lapse between one attack and the next— thus ♪ 𝄾 , ♪ 𝄾 𝄾 , ♪♪𝄾 (triplet), ♪. 𝄾 , and ♩ are each equivalent to one quarter-note value):

1. 𝅗𝅥 (bars 4 and 5); ♩.. ; (bar 6); ♩ ♪ (bar 6); ♩ (bar 7); ♩ 𝄾 (triplet 3) (bar 8)
2. 𝅗𝅥 (bar 10); ♩. (bar 11); ♩ (bar 11); ♪. (bar 14); ♪ (bar 17)

Note that the new and shorter note values are almost invariably introduced on the way to a new pitch climax, after which they recede. Note also that this effect is cumulative, though not consistently so. In (1) above:

One ♩ in bar 7 en route to high E

Two ♩♪'s in bar 8 en route to high E♭
    3

In (2) above:

Three ♩'s in bars 11 and 12 en route to high F

Four ♩.'s in bars 14 and 15 en route to high B

Motivic Manipulation

Both composers place severe limitations on their aural building blocks. Bach limits himself to three tiny rhythmic cells and their manipulation through variation and reordering. Carter limits himself to three intervals (M2, m2, and A4), plus their manipulation by reordering and by octave transposition of tones. The lower staves in Example 4.12 show all the tones of the Carter melody with octave transpositions reduced to the smallest interval size. The brackets reveal an underlying motive which embodies the three intervals.

This underlying motive, never heard in its basic simplicity, appears in four forms, invariably transposed (Ex. 4.13). Within these forms, m2 and M2 are often reversed in order. Sometimes two or three of the tones are heard simultaneously, and sometimes m2 or M3 is missing—consistently in bars 15 through 18—throwing the unsettling tritone into clearer focus. The motive almost always overlaps not only itself but the phrase breaks as well. There is a notable exception in bar 13, emphasizing the dominant.

4.13

The underlying motive stakes out the aural limits. Its various manipulations contribute to the subtle though powerful climactic forces that sum up the onward urgency and the expressive power of the melody. Each of those climactic forces reaches its apex well into the latter half of the melody, but those apexes do not necessarily coincide:

Diminution (quantitative—four consecutive ♩.'s) in bars 14 and 15
Range (highest pitch) in bar 16
Diminution (qualitative—shortest value ♪) in bar 17
Motivic overlap in bar 17
Intervalic tension (tritone emphasis) in bars 15 to 19
Range (lowest pitch) in bar 19
Tonic emphasis in bars 19 and 20

Perhaps some of the factors we have just been considering in the Carter melody could be construed as vestiges of the eighteenth-century practices of Bach and his contemporaries. In the larger view they represent something a great deal more meaningful: the continuing evolution of musical materials and their use—a long line which no composer has ever successfully broken.

Don't let your study of melodies stop here. Rather, let every melody you encounter—not excluding your favorite popular songs—be subjected to the same sort of structural scrutiny we have applied to the five in this chapter.

MAKING YOUR MELODY

If you have noticed that in none of the melodies we have just dissected have the composers faithfully heeded the rules you have had to follow in making models, don't feel resentful. As you read earlier, any set of rules is less binding for the mature composer than the self-imposed limitations of his own aesthetic aims of the moment. Principles tend for the most part to remain constant while rules are expendable—sometimes perhaps disconcertingly so.

As you have no doubt anticipated, models will serve as guidelines for your melodies. For semantic convenience, a melody will often be referred to as a *decoration* of the model. That term is only partially apt, however. I like to think of this part of your work as learning how to imbue a spare and skeletal, though purposeful, design with communicable character and dynamic vitality. In this, your methods will hardly differ from those of the mature composer. For it is difficult to imagine anyone setting out to make a melody without having at least intuitively in mind certain goal tones, areas, shapes, tonal organizations, and means of propulsion. So that you will have clean and tidy habits from the beginning, the model will supply most of these, as will the second and third voices later on.

Here are three important ways in which your melody will relate to your model:

1. The tones of the model will be the principal stress tones of the melody.
2. The tones which define the shape of the model (first tone, last tone, and climax tones) will usually, if not invariably, perform the same service for the melody.
3. The tones of the model which control the tonal center will carry that function into your melody.

Thus the principal *structural* elements are, so to speak, built in. The rest is squarely up to your developing imagination and ingenuity! This means, more specifically, the invention and logical development of the motives. Your very first attempts might be more coherent, at least superficially, if I furnished you with step-by-step rules for this enterprise. I quite emphatically refrain from this procedure.

Good melodies are not made merely by piecing together motives, cells, phrases, step-progressions, tonal centers, etc., any more than a mechanical combination of letters, words, phrases, clauses, sentences, paragraphs, and punctuation marks can even suggest, let alone ensure, a good essay in English. Our analysis should not have fostered that impression, for analysis is not composition. It is the exact opposite: its function is to expose coherent thought.

Good melodies, like good essays, flow from coherent thought. The motive is the germ of that thought. So invent your motive and carry on from there with its development. Our analysis has given you some principles and precedents. Play your melody over and over again during and after its composition. Be ruthlessly self-critical. Avoid the pitfall of accepting something as good just because repeated playings have accustomed you to the pattern. Hard listening will help you to detect any gaps in thought coherence. *Then* the precedents uncovered by our analysis can come to your aid in closing these gaps.

Nevertheless, here are some things you should bear in mind while writing your melodies:

1. The first motive should be in some way memorable in materials and character. Factors which contribute to memorability are:
   a. easily recognizable rhythmic cell or cells
   b. striking if simple contour
   c. limitation to a very few intervals which can be perceived as characteristic

Obviously *all* motives need not depend on all three of these factors!

2. Any subsequent motive, or motives, should be in some way contrasted to the first—but not so wildly contrasted as to deny a sense of relationship.
3. The number of motives should be severely limited—very seldom more than two or three. This is to encourage a sense of concentration.
4. Some of your earlier melodies may very well be no more than a single phrase in length. When you employ two or more phrases try to make each phrase inevitably follow and "explain" its predecessor by means of the binding forces discussed above—particularly step-progressions that span the clearly defined phrase breaks.

A few specific notes about the handling of tones. In this, you can be a bit freer than in the construction of the model, since the model itself already gives certain structural and aesthetic assurances.

5. The last tone may be approached by any interval, provided the last two tones of the *model* carry enough stress to confirm the tonal center.
6. All intervals are available, but bear in mind that:
   a. large interval skips tend to demand a subsequent change of direction, usually to a tone within the skip;
   b. skips of tense intervals tend to require at least eventual satisfaction by way of resolution;
   c. The sense of orientation to the model tones should not be overwhelmed.
7. Repeated tones, chord outlines, contiguous leaps, sequences, scale passages, chromatics, augmented and diminished intervals, and more than four tones without a change of direction are permissible. While these formulations would be disruptive to the function of the model if incorporated in it, they can be useful expressive and structural factors in its decoration. But use restraint! You must be able to sing it.

Example 4.14 is the same model that opened Chapter 3, and Examples 4.15 to 4.19 show several specimen decorations of this model. It will be seen that the model exhibits some obvious step-progressions. This is not surprising, since it is itself a skeletal melody.

These step-progressions will inevitably affect the coherence of the decoration melody. (Notice that the model is transposed down a whole tone in Ex. 4.16 and up a tone in Ex. 4.17. This, of course, does not affect the relationship of the tones to each other within the model.)

4.14

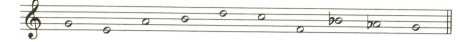

Example 4.15 uses only one very simple motive, seeking variety through its variation. The second appearance of the motive is an inversion of the first, and eliminates the tie. The third shows three quarter-notes where there had been only one. The last two are slight rhythmic variations—squeezing or stretching a note. The last employs a half note for the Ab, since that note, being a model tone, is to be stressed, while the motivically comparable F in the second bar merely passes stepwise between two stress notes. This, however, is turned to expressive ends by way of braking the action after the veritable flurry (!) of activity in bar 7. Only three notes are added to those already present in the model. The bracket below the line embraces what sounds almost like a second motive; actually it is a rhythmic retrograde.

4.15

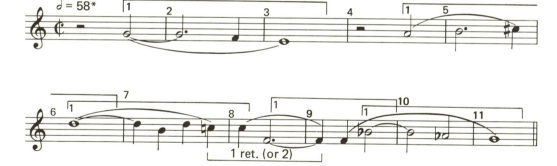

Example 4.16 uses no tones other than model tones, though two pairs of these are repeated. Motive 1 is really nothing more than a characteristic rhythm. It is incomplete in its last two appearances. Motive 2, while in contrast to 1, is related to it by virtue of the identical time lapse between the first two accented C's in bar three and the second and third notes of motive 1 (and also the offbeat final Gb).

*Such things as tempo indications, phrase markings, dynamic symbols, and articulation marks should all be included in the notation of your melodies. A useful reference book in this connection is Carl A. Rosenthal's *Practical Guide to Music Notation,* New York, 1967.

4.16

In Example 4.17, the means of giving stress are repetition and duration; those tones stressed by duration are always preceded by an accented note which "leans into" it, thereby adding the stress of resolution (except in bars 2 and 7—why?). In bars 5 and 6 the leaning characteristic of motive 2 is incorporated into motive 1 to intensify the motivic interest in the climax area by telescoping the rhythmic characteristics of the two motives.

4.17

Example 4.18 is a bit more elaborate, not in its motivic structure but in its supplementation of the original notes of the model. The upper and lower climaxes are each extended a half-step beyond those of the model, slightly weakening the tonal stability—a process which is aided somewhat by the "wandering" in bar 3 and the "cancellation" of the tonic by the G♭ (as part of a simple triad) in bar 5. Note in bar 4 the ministep-progression, D-C-B♭, which after the long B♭ is echoed in bar 5 by the much quicker D♭-C-B♭. This functions as a binding force here, particularly since that kind of three-tone cell is present elsewhere in varying degrees of clarity. Some of these are marked below the staff. Find others. Note also the step-progression from E in bar 2 up to D (dominant) in bar 4.

4.18

The final decoration (Ex. 4.19) is constructed a little differently from the others. Each of the model tones is either the first or the last tone of a phrase. Each is further stressed by duration in relation to the intervening tones in each phrase. Many of them have additional stresses. The primary shape tones, other than the tonic, are not model tones. Note the other step-progressions in addition to those already provided by the tones of the model. All but two of the melodic progressions are by large skip. Motive coincides with phrase. The motive is identified chiefly by its rhythmic structure—one to three short notes between the longer first and last notes. The overall rhythmic method is that of intensification by contraction. Each phrase is shorter than the one before it, as are the notes themselves by comparison with those in corresponding positions in the previous phrase. So there is something of a rush to "spit out" the last and shortest phrase.

4.19

Now make melodies—all kinds of melodies—basing them on your old models or on new ones. (It is sometimes a good idea to make several decorations of the same model, all different in character, even wildly so.) If you have never made a melody before and don't know how to get started, don't worry—just start. Make slow melodies, fast melodies, light melodies, serious melodies, romantic melodies, amusing melodies, stark melodies, lush melodies, "safe" melodies, experimental melodies, "far out" melodies. In short, make melodies!

5 THE TWO-VOICE STRUCTURE

We now proceed to study the art of combining one melody with another. This art of controlled purposeful polyphony has long occupied a position of particular glory in the history of Western music, and high skills as well as inspiration are requisite to its successful practice. The rudiments of those skills can be acquired here, but the inspiration will come only from total surrender to the tasks and pleasures of the effort, and a constant insistence on your part that each exercise contain at least some tiny seed of beauty.

Up to this point you have been concerned exclusively with a single horizontal line or melody which is substantially a law unto itself, free of exterior restraints. Your task now is not only to make two such melodies, but also to create a reciprocal relationship between them which adds up to something more than just the sum of the two parts. This relationship should clearly identify the two equally independent voices, it should establish a clear and constant tonal direction, and it should create a span of interest and tension from beginning to end which gives the listener (as did the model itself) a definite starting point, an "elastic stretching" departure, and a final, acceptable goal.

THE SECOND VOICE

We begin by writing a new model precisely as we wrote models in Chapter 3. This will be the first voice, which is *never* changed, and which is called hereafter, as heretofore, the "model." The second voice, like the model, is written in whole notes—one to go with each note of the model—and it can be placed either above the model or below it. You should give equal attention to both distributions. Write at least one second voice above each model and at least one below it. In fact, if you are really intent on developing your skill with tones, try to exhaust the second-voice possibilities of each model, but keep only those which are the most satisfying to the ear in fulfilling the aims, and determine what points contribute to their superiority. Some models will, of course, accommodate a greater variety of second voices than others, though I have still to find a model for which suitable second voices cannot be found.

As you read the above, you no doubt perceived that the possibilities may be rather severely limited. This is true because the second voice must accommodate itself to the already existing and unchangeable model even while following precisely the same set of rules that governed the construction of that model—with three exceptions:

1. The approach to the final tone may be by any major, minor, or perfect interval which is no larger than P5. This allows the second voice four final progressions denied to the model (Ex. 5.1). This is feasible because, unless some other two-voice rule is violated, the model's cadence, already present and unchangeable, assures sufficient strength in the cadential progression, as in Example 5.2.
2. When the second voice is placed *above* the model it need not (although it may) begin and end on the same tone. The only requirement, in the interest of tonal coherence, is that the final diad be one with its root on the bottom. That root is, of course, the last tone of the model and the tonic of the entire two-voice structure (Ex. 5.3).

5.1

5.2

5.3

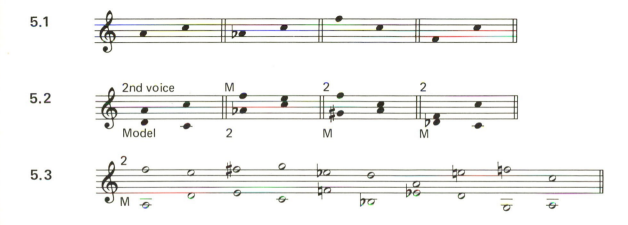

Quite obviously, placing the second voice below the model could establish in the two-voice structure a tonic other than that of the model. In any case, if the second voice is *below* the model, it *must* begin and end on the same tone, which must be the root of the interval formed by that tone and the model's tonic. That final tone of the second voice is then the tonic of the completed two-voice structure. In Example 5.4a, the tonic is that of the model, but in Example 5.4b, the tonic becomes that of the second voice.

a *Second voice below—model tonic retained in two-voice structure*

5.4

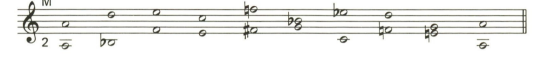

b *Second voice below—new tonic in two-voice structure*

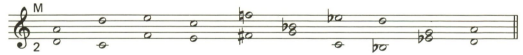

3. Though the second voice, because of its tonal interaction with the model, can tolerate repeated tones a little more readily than the model itself, any one of the following three progressions must take place before a tone may be repeated:

   a. as in the model, two skips with roots other than the tone repeated (see Ex. 3.19)

   b. an augmented unison properly resolved, plus *at least* one skip whose root is a tone other than the repeated one (Ex. 5.5)

   c. when absolutely necessary, an augmented unison, properly resolved, of which the repeated tone is itself one of the members (Ex. 5.6)

Even compliance with one or more of these three conditions may not erase the ritarding effect of the repetition if the tone repeated has additional strong support within or outside the group.

The discussion of the second voice itself has already touched on the relationship between the two voices. The material on which that relationship rests consists of all the intervals shown in Example 2.3 and all other augmented and diminished intervals. Since the two-voice structure places one note above or below each tone of the model, it will consist of the same number of diads as there are tones in the model. *All* intervals are available for these diads. It is possible that the more stable intervals will predominate as vertical relationships between simultaneously sounding tones. However, expediency or taste—perhaps both—will often dictate the use of more tense intervals which, of course, require immediate resolution (see Ex. 2.4 and the discussion that accompanies it).

INDEPENDENCE OF VOICES

You will recall from the second paragraph of this chapter that one of the requirements of the two-voice structure is the clear identification of each voice. To this end certain precautions need to be taken.

Range

The first of these has to do with range. The second voice, like the model, will be sung by untrained voices, and therefore its range should never be more than slightly over an octave. It is suggested that the two-voice structure—for purposes of clarity—be written for two different voices, such as soprano-alto, alto-tenor, tenor-bass, soprano-tenor, alto-bass, or soprano-bass. For each voice the range limit of your fellow students will be quickly determined as they begin to sing your work in class.

Voice Crossings and Overlaps

The second precaution for ensuring clarity prohibits crossing the two voices. This, of course, does not mean their ranges may not overlap, but simply that at all times the tone sounding in the upper voice must be higher than the one sounding simultaneously in the lower voice.

The Motions

The third precaution has to do with the *motions.* These are defined as the directions in which the two voices move in progressing from one diad to the next. There are four of them:

1. *Oblique* (O)—one voice remaining stationary, the other moving in either direction (Ex. 5.7). (For obvious reasons, oblique motion is not a consideration in this chapter.)
2. *Contrary* (C)—the two voices moving in opposite directions (Ex. 5.8)
3. *Similar* (S)—the two voices moving in the same direction to a second interval different in size from the first (Ex. 5.9)
4. *Parallel* (P)—the two voices moving in the same direction to an interval identical in size to the first (Ex. 5.10)

5.7

5.8

5.9

5.10

A preponderance of similar or parallel motions produces a mildly ludicrous "cat-and-mouse" effect (Ex. 5.11), while an overemphasis on contrary motion spawns a too-predictable "mirror" effect (Ex. 5.12). To enhance the individuality of each voice, the two-voice structure should strike a judicious balance between the motions, as in Example 5.13.

5.11

5.12

5.13

Combining as they do the harmonic strength of a skip with the melodic suavity of a step, progressions in which one voice moves by step while the other moves by skip tend to provide a special satisfaction. The generous use of such progressions, as in Example 5.14, is therefore encouraged.

5.14

In the final progression of the two-voice structure, only one of the voices may move by skip. This rule does *not*, of course, prevent both voices from moving by step.

Parallels

Parallel perfect intervals are never used in the two-voice structure. The domination of these intervals by their roots all but reduces one of the voices to a shadow of the other. The effect is equally bad if one of the intervals is compounded (Ex. 5.15). In any case, parallel intervals of any size tend to detract from vocal independence if for no other reason than lack of variety, as in Example 5.16, or lack of beauty and clarity of progression, as in Example 5.17. You are enjoined only against using parallel *perfect* intervals, but think twice before using *any* parallels.

5.15

5.16

5.17

Simultaneous Leaps

Likewise, both voices skipping simultaneously in similar or parallel motion produce a parasitic effect which borders on parody and is therefore to be avoided (Ex. 5.18).

5.18

Climaxes

At least one other factor can influence the independence of the voices—melodic climaxes. You have already learned that the model has either an upper or a lower climax, or both. The same is true, of course, of the second voice. This means that each of your two-voice structures will embrace two to four such climaxes (Ex. 5.19). Try to avoid the temporal coincidence of any of these, especially the "outside" ones, that is, the upper climax of the upper voice and the lower climax of the lower voice. (See Ex. 5.13, however, for a comparatively harmless coincidence of climaxes.)

5.19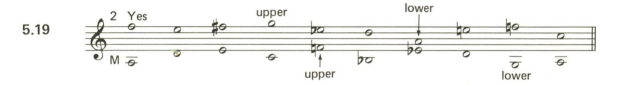

*Note that this progression does not constitute a crossing of voices—merely an overlapping.

A brief reference to principle may be appropriate here. You may well be aware, now or in the future, of the compositional technique which brings all factors to bear on a single temporal point for climactic purposes. It is very likely that you will at some time employ this technique. If the caution against a coincidence of climaxes seems to dispute it, please recall patiently that these two-voice structures are not really compositions but training in elementary techniques. In a composition embracing one or more such single temporal points, there are sure to be countless other points which display no such convergence of factors. Our goal here is maximum independence of the two voices rather than their even momentary cooperation in some other enterprise!

CLEAR AND CONSTANT TONAL DIRECTION

We seek independence for each of the voices, and we also seek a similar degree of self-determination for each of the diads in the two-voice structure. This means that each progression from one diad to the next must accomplish one or both of the following: it must bring about a clear and unmistakable change of root and, insofar as possible, it must regale the ear with fresh tones.

Four kinds of progressions can frustrate these aims and should, therefore, be avoided. The effects produced by these formulations are among the most difficult to perceive, since they require you to listen in a way that you may not have consciously listened before—backward, if you like—instinctively and sensitively relating what you *are* hearing to what you *have been* hearing. Those grouped under (1) and (2) in the list which follows are the most likely to slip past you in the beginning, simply because they can sound so common and reasonable that you are not prompted to stop and realize exactly *what they do.* Past aural experience may not often lead you initially into traps such as those shown later in Example 5.25, because seconds, sevenths, and ninths in similar or parallel motion, while certainly permissible in context, may not tempt you aesthetically at first. Here are the formulations to be avoided:

1. Any progression in which *all four tones,* when sounded simultaneously, adhere unmistakably to a single root by virtue of acoustical simplicity or psychological habit—that is, an exchange of tones, triads consisting of superimposed major and/or minor thirds, and seventh chords which contain a tritone. Example 5.20 shows a few of these progressions.

5.20

2. Any progression employing *exclusively,* both vertically and horizontally, M2, M3, and A4 or the inversion of any of them. The tritone, unopposed by a half-step progression, is here the binding force in its demand for resolution. Among these particular dangers to intervallic self-determination, the easiest to spot as you work is the kind shown in Example 5.21.

5.21

Progressions such as those in Example 5.22, however, are no less disrupting to clear root progression.

5.22

Enharmonic spelling of one or more of the intervals does not alter the effect of disruption (the d4 and A5 in Ex. 5.23 *sound* like M3 and m6, and for practical aural calculations *are* M3 and m6).

5.23

3. Any progression in which both intervals have, or could have, the same root (Ex. 5.24).

5.24

4. Any progressions comprising two intervals with comparatively ambiguous roots. Such progressions require special care in order to ensure a sense of motion and direction. These intervals are m2 and M2; to a lesser degree m9 and M9; and to a still lesser degree M7 and m7. Since a pair of ambiguously rooted intervals could hardly be expected to produce a strong progression of roots, the sense of motion must depend rather heavily on the introduction of fresh tones in the second diad of such progressions. Therefore, try insofar as possible to avoid anticipations like those marked with dotted lines in Example 5.25.

5.25

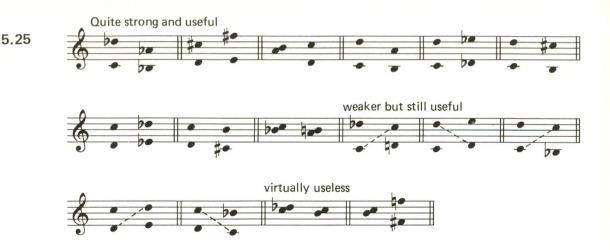

In connection with anticipations: no tone of the lower voice should ever be anticipated *in the same octave* by the other voice (Ex. 5.26). (You would never write the last progression in Example 5.26 in any case. Why not?)

5.26

If the progressions in Example 5.20 to 5.26 seem labyrinthine in their kinds and number of proscriptions, take comfort from the fact that for every forbidden progression there are dozens of good and useful ones.

SPAN OF INTEREST AND TENSION

The third general aim of the two-voice structure—the creation of a span of controlled interest and tension from beginning to end—may very well be the most important one. It depends partly, of course, on the successful achievement of the other aims, but it is the accomplishment of this last aim that can render a two-voice structure capable of returning some degree of aesthetic satisfaction even within its narrow scope.

First of all, as you did in the model, avoid emphasizing the tonic except at the very beginning and at the cadence. A diad whose root is the tonic will not ordinarily disrupt the tonal flow *if that root is in the upper voice.*

Next, try to employ a variety of vertical intervals, just for the sake of the minute surprises this effort can yield. Look back at Example 2.3: each of the intervals there is, of course, perfectly acceptable in its sound, though the quality of each is unique—sometimes only subtly so in comparison with those on either side of it.

The perfect intervals have great tonal stability but are rather hollow and bland in sonority. An unbroken series of them is apt to be somewhat less than satisfying in sound (Ex. 5.27).

5.27

The major and minor thirds and sixths, tonally somewhat less stable than the perfect intervals, stimulate the ear because they verge on greater tension. Perhaps the reason they are such useful intervals is that they are relatively noncommittal in the direction of either stability or tension.

The intervals of tension, through their relative harshness as well as their comparative tonal instability, can contribute to the two-voice structure not only because of their purely sonic interest but also because they render the stability of the final cadence all the more welcome. They can serve as the delicious pepper that makes the sneeze so satisfying! Precise placement of the tense intervals during the course of the two-voice structure may be crucial. From Bach at least through Schoenberg the greatest concentrations of tension were most often reserved for two places—the penultimate chord of the phrase and the climactic points. This principle is still valid, though various means besides intervallic tension have been increasingly employed to fulfill it, including some extremes of textural complexity and decibelic pandemonium.

Perfect Intervals

Particular care is needed in handling the perfect (ultrastable) intervals. You remember that the model begins with the tonic but, until the very end, refrains from further emphasis on that note lest the tension be prematurely dispelled. To a lesser degree, the span of interest and tension in the two-voice structure can be similarly broken by over-emphasis on one or another of the perfect intervals.

Covered Perfect Fifths and Fourths

A P5 or a P4 is called a *covered* P5 or P4 if it is approached in similar motion, as in Example 5.28. All the progressions shown in this example are perfectly useful in the two-voice structure except the two marked No. If P5 or P4 is approached in *upward* similar motion, the upper voice should never skip. Overemphasis is thus to a large degree avoided. Play the progressions in this example. Can you hear the difference between them?

5.28

If P5 or P4 is approached by step from below, the upper voice should move by half-step. Example 5.29 shows both unacceptable and acceptable approaches.

5.29

Covered, hidden, and *direct* are the adjectives traditionally used to describe perfect intervals which are approached in similar motion, upward *or* downward. Only the approaches proscribed above need be avoided.

Covered Octaves and Unisons

For reasons which surely no longer need explanation, overemphasis on any single tone is undesirable in any spot other than the final cadence, where such strength may be just the proper thing. The similar motion by which covered octaves and unisons are approached does propel the attention toward a single tone. Therefore, covered octaves and unisons are used only at the cadence, as in Example 5.30a. Even then, the upper voice may not skip upward. Such a skip creates an emphasis which is not only strong, but also overobvious, sonically bland, and banal (Ex. 5.30b).

5.30

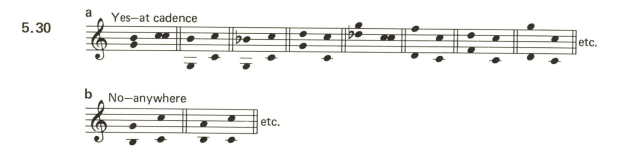

Note: Octaves and unisons, while *permissible* as vertical relationships when absolutely necessary in the course of the two-voice structure, are intervals containing essentially only one tone. Surrounded in the structure by sonically superior two-tone diads, they are apt to fare badly in comparison, even when approached by contrary motion. Therefore, except in the final diad, they should be thought of as havens of very last resort (Ex. 5.31)!

5.31

* At best, the last two progressions in Example 5.29 are of questionable value *in two voices,* and should be used only as a last resort. Why?

The Perfect Fourth

The perfect fourth, like other perfect intervals, is so stable and positive in its root delineation that the root all but gobbles up the other, nonroot, tone. The root of P4 is, of course, the upper tone. This puts the already obliterated nonroot tone in the lowest voice, charging it with the responsibility of supporting the sonority. In context, it quite understandably tends to buckle beneath its burden. You can and should alleviate this burden by careful approach and departure; in each of these progressions at least one of the voices must move by step, as in Example 5.32.

5.32

The Augmented Octave and Unison

One more source of interest and tension in the two-voice structure is the augmented or diminished octave and the augmented unison. These are, of course, among the intervals available as vertical relationships and, as tense intervals, they are subject to immediate resolution as discussed in Chapter 2. However, if only one of the tones in such an interval appears in either of the voices, its resolution must occur *in that same voice and in that same octave* before, or simultaneously with, the introduction of the other member *in either voice in any octave* (Ex. 5.33; see also Ex. 3.13).

5.33

It is safe to say that, if you observe all these precautions, you can make a good second voice, whether above or below, for any model. Tenacity in perceiving and trying out all possibilities is the answer to all problems. If you should be so unlucky as to come up with one of those very rare models which seem to defy every second-voice possibility, an adjustment in the form of an outlined triad in the second voice may be in order. This will involve—*as a last resort only*—momentarily setting aside rule 9 (see Appendix I).

Make a number of two-voice structures. (You will often find it fruitful to begin by making several possible final cadences, working backward from each, and finally selecting the best result.)

Proceed no further until you can depend on your ability to make second voices that are free of errors. You will then be ready to start persuading the tones to do your bidding.

CONTROL OF ALL FACTORS

The Melodic Line

Concentrate first on the melodic line, making several examples in which you strive for linear grace and interest. The aesthetic judgments called into play here are hardly subject to rules beyond those given for the model in Chapter 3, but they *are* subject to the increasingly informed opinions of you and your fellow students as well as those of your instructor. Scrutinize your work very carefully and critically in classroom performance.

Intervallic Tension

In two voices, as you may soon discover, there is not much latitude for the precise control of tension. Such control must be reserved largely for the work in three voices, to be discussed in Chapters 7 and 8. This is why you have been told, in the interest of sonic unity, that vertical intervals of comparative stability will usually predominate. You can, however, experiment with the best placement of those tense intervals which you may choose or be forced to use. In general, try to place them where they will do the most good—in and just before the cadence progression, or at climaxes. The following list will refer you back to the examples in this chapter that demonstrate the use of tense intervals at these points:

1. At the cadence area—Examples 5.11, 5.13, 5.19
2. At melodic climaxes generally—Examples 5.3, 5.4, 5.11
3. At the upper and lower climaxes of the lower voice—Example 5.19
4. At the upper climax of the upper voice—Example 5.4a and b (each shows one or two tense intervals pushing toward the upper climax); Example 5.19 (diads 2 and 3 push toward the upper climax)
5. At the upper and lower climaxes of the upper voice—Example 5.11

Make some two-voice structures in which your first priority is placement of the tense intervals. Mark each interval as follows:

>   0 for stable interval (mark may be omitted)
>   1 for M2 or inversion
>   2 for m2 or inversion
>   3 for A4 or d5

All the remaining structures in this chapter are so marked.

The Tonal Center

In the two-voice structure, your control of the strength of the tonal center is, of course, affected by the tonal characteristics of the two horizontal lines themselves. If the model, for instance, were to consist only of the tones of one of the old tonal scales, it would not be easy to destroy that habitual orientation to its tonic. In addition, if the cadence is a strong one (subdominant-dominant-tonic, for example), the tonic would tend to predominate even more.

If the model, on the other hand, were shot through with some of the various factors which weaken the tonal center to a marked degree (see Ex. 3.40b to 3.42), then it would be difficult (although not always impossible) to strengthen the tonic by various means. It is to be assumed, however, that in the interest of stylistic integrity a strongly tonic-oriented model would suggest a similarly oriented two-voice structure, and that a model verging on atonality would be most happy in a two-voice structure which sensitively heeded its inherent characteristics.

At this point you would do well to review Chapter 3 from page 32 to the end. As you do this, bear in mind that the placement of tonal functions is the real determinant of tonic power. In the model this power is expressed by the presence or absence of functional tones themselves (D, S, T, and L), by skips which have these tones for their roots, and by the positioning of these tones and skips.

In the two-voice structure, control of the tonal center also depends heavily on the presence, absence, and position of these same functional tones. But in the two-voice structure these tonal functions are expressed mainly by the roots of the diads.

Therefore, the surest way to make a two-voice structure with a strong tonic is to concentrate a number of function-rooted diads in the cadence area, and the surest way to weaken the tonic is to avoid those functions, particularly at the end and at the beginning.

The structure in Example 5.34a uses only the tones of the G major scale, and the functions are bunched at the cadence. The result is an irrevocable tonic.

Example 5.34b has the same scalar model (transposed) and the same functional placement as (a), but here the tonic is weakened slightly by two chromatics (Bb-♮, C♮-♯). (Notice how the tension in the penultimate diad strengthens the cadence.)

Again, Example 5.34c uses the same scalar model (transposed) as in (a) and (b), but now the tonic is virtually bereft of functional support. The tonic is further weakened by placement of tension—compare with (b)—and still further weakened by four chromatics (E♯-♮, F𝄪-♯, D♯-♮, C♯-♮).

5.34

In Example 5.35a, the model is scalar (descending minor), and the functions are strongly placed. Though the cadence is strengthened by tension placement, the tonic is slightly weakened by two chromatics (A♯-♮, E♮-♯).

Example 5.35b has the same scalar model and almost the same functional support as in (a). Here, however, the cadence is somewhat weakened by tension placement, and the three chromatics (B♭-♮, C♯-♮, F♮-♯) produce a weaker tonic than in (a). This structure uses a total of ten tones.

Example 5.35c uses the same scalar model as (a) and (b), but with a new tonic. The functional support is about equal to that in (a) and (b), but less strategically placed. Though the cadence is strengthened by tension placement, it is weaker than in (a) and (b) by virtue of replacement of the dominant with the upper leading tone.

5.35

> Make a model using conventional scales and strong harmonic cadential functions.
> Then make two second voices for it—one which confirms the scale and the cadence
> functions, and one which negates them to the limit of aesthetic acceptability.

The model in Example 5.36a is nonscalar, with harmonic functions bunched at the cadence. Functional support, except at the cadence, is very weak, though tension strengthens the tonic (and cadence). Eleven tones are used.

Example 5.36b uses the same model as (a), with a new tonic. Leading-tone functional support is only minimal, and the cadential functional support in the model is negated, though the cadence benefits by the tension in the penultimate diad. Again, eleven tones are used.

5.36

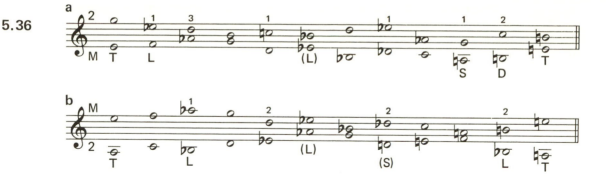

In Example 5.37a, the model again has a strong functional cadence (S-D-T), and the structure conforms to those functions. Eleven tones are used.

Example 5.37b shows one good way to kill the strong cadential functions of the model:

1. The new tonic (E?) is ambiguous to begin with because of the uncertain root of M2.
2. All other functions (or nearly all) are equally ambiguous—even questionable.
3. All twelve tones are used, with all the chromatics that this implies.

5.37

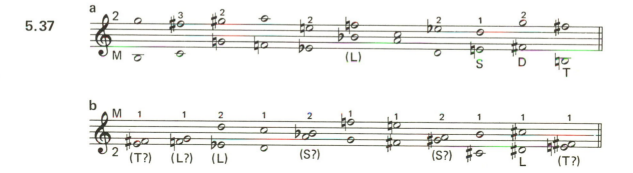

> Make some models which, insofar as possible, minimize tonic support right up to the cadence. The cadence, however, is to have strong harmonic functional support. Make several second voices for each model, with each second voice further under-cutting that cadential support.

The model in Example 5.38a sacrifices some tonic strength through the placement of the harmonic functions at the beginning rather than at the end. The structure merely confirms the functions of the model.

Example 5.38b, while displaying fewer harmonic functions than (a), shows a slightly stronger tonic by virtue of the leading-tone function actually adjacent to the final tonic. There are also more stable intervals.

Of the three structures in Example 5.38, (c) has the strongest tonic by virtue of the strategic placement of the functional tones.

5.38

Make some models that have strong functional support at the beginning which weakens thereafter. Then, experiment by using these models in structures which strengthen or weaken the tonic in varying degrees.

The tonic of the model in Example 5.39a has no strong harmonic functional support—actually the only direct functional support is the leading tone at the cadence. The two-voice structure adds little to the tonic strength, and the tension in the last diad detracts from that strength.

Example 5.39b has the same weaker-tonic model as (a), but the structure produces a new tonic made comparatively strong by means of a strategically placed dominant.

5.39

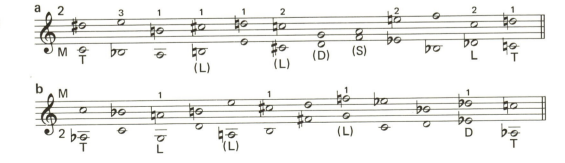

> Make some models whose only strategic functional support is the upper or lower
> leading tone. Through the second voices, experiment with strong and weak tonics.

The models in Examples 5.40 and 5.41, as well as those in the remaining structures in
this chapter, are designed with tonic ambiguity in mind. The structures are designed to
reinforce these ambiguities. For instance, the dominants in Examples 5.40 and 5.41 are
in parentheses because there is no possibility of their being felt as such at the time they
are heard.

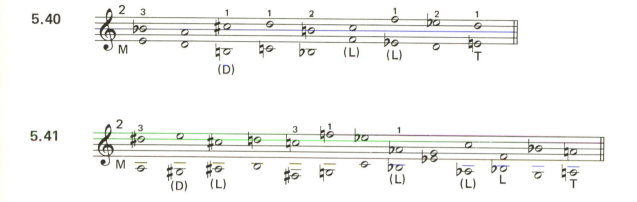

> Make some models with as little direct functional support for the tonic as possible.
> Make some second voices which confirm that nonsupport, others which seek as
> strong a tonic as possible.

The models in the two structures of Example 5.42 exploit the exceptions to rule 6
(see Appendix 1), and in each the second voice adds further ambiguities.

The models in the structures of Example 5.43 (from Ex. 3.42c and d) use the first exception to rule 6 at the cadence. Again, the addition of the second voice does little or nothing in support of the tonic. Note the outlined seventh chord in (b), hardly disastrous in the highly fluid tonal context.

5.43

Make some models which employ as many exceptions to rule 6 as possible. Construct second voices which render the tonic utterly ambiguous except for the fact that it is the last root to be heard. Then make others which seek as clear a tonic as possible.

Perhaps you can see that the important part of your work comes after completion of the comparatively easy task of mastering the rules. It consists in learning to exercise purposeful controls with specific aims in view but without predetermined answers or outcomes—just as in the case of the mature composer. Never mind if your work must seem naive and elementary by comparison. Remember that if the steps to Parnassus in composition were numbered, there could be no steps 998, 999, and 1000 without steps 1, 2, and 3! And remember too that while not all musicians can negotiate all those steps, you and every other musician should negotiate as many of them as time and talent permit.

SUGGESTED READING

Johann Joseph Fux: *Steps to Parnassus*
Paul Hindemith: *Exercises in Two-Part Writing*
Jean-Philippe Rameau: *Treatise on Harmony*

6 TWO MELODIES

This chapter relates to Chapter 5 in the same way that Chapter 4 related to Chapter 3. The procedure will be the same except that instead of decorating the single-line model as in Chapter 4, we will decorate both voices of the two-voice structure in such a way that the two melodies will enhance each other.

Example 6.1 shows a typical two-voice structure, and Examples 6.2 to 6.7 are six decorations of this structure, showing some of the endless ways in which two melodies can enhance each other. The upper voice in Example 6.2, for instance, has been decorated to form quite an elaborate melody, supported by a lower voice which is decorated hardly at all. These two roles might be reversed, as in Example 6.3. Example 6.4 shows how one voice might support the other by virtue of their very similarity, while in Example 6.5 the two voices complement each other by a kind of rhythmic give-and-take. The two voices could run along simultaneously, as in Example 6.6, with no more than minimal overt recognition of each other's existence—rather like two young children playing *alongside* each other rather than *with* each other. On the other hand, the voices might be in open conflict, as in the final decoration in Example 6.7.

The possibilities, of which Examples 6.2 to 6.7 represent only a few, are almost limitless, but they all have at least one thing in common: the two melodies, being "partners" in musical expression, must accommodate themselves to each other in several ways—in harmony, range, motive, rhythm, phrase, texture, etc. The study and practice of these accommodations is the business of this chapter.

6.1

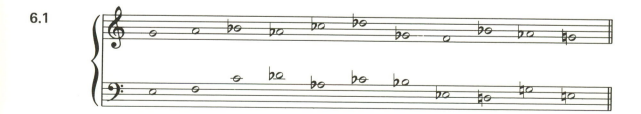

6.2

6.3

6.4

6.5

6.6

6.7

GENERAL PROCEDURE

The two melodies are made by decorating each of the voices of the two-voice structure, and the tones of each of these voices serve as the principal stress tones in the corresponding melodies—exactly as in Chapter 4.

At least for the present, each diad of the two-voice structure, and hence the decorations of its two tones, will occupy one measure. The measures may be of any length you choose —$\frac{4}{4}, \frac{3}{4}, \frac{6}{8}, \frac{9}{8}, \frac{2}{4}, \frac{5}{8}, \frac{7}{4}$, etc. All the measures will probably, but need not, be of equal length.

At least in the beginning, write all your melodies so that they can be easily sung in class—and be sure to sing them there. Later, when you are technically secure, write some of them as little duets for whatever instruments are available in class. In this way you will begin to acquire some knowledge of instrumentation—the most reliable sort of knowledge, because of the immediate practical testing it will receive.

DECORATING THE UPPER VOICE

We will proceed by decorating first the upper voice. The object, of course, is to make a good melody that, as far as possible, will sound free and unfettered by other considerations. However, unlike the decorations you did in Chapter 5, these melodies must be written with due respect for the limitations imposed by the presence of another voice or melody. The first of these limitations is brought about by the vertical (harmonic) implications of each of the diads in the two-voice structure.

While it is true that in decorating the upper voice the upper tone of each diad is to receive more stress than any other melody tone in that voice in that measure, other tones are, of course, available. These fall into two categories—chord tones and auxiliary tones.

Stable Chord Tones

The *chord tones* in any given measure are those that neither perceptibly disturb nor replace the original or the chosen root of the diad. In the beginning, the chord tones added to the diad tones for decoration will be only stable ones; that is, they must meet two requirements:

1. They will have the same root as the root of the diad, as in Example 6.8, or, if another root is chosen, they will have that chosen tone as root, as in Example 6.9.
2. They will all form stable intervals with their root, though not necessarily with the other diad tone.

6.8

6.9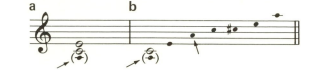

Care should be taken, if a root other than the original one is chosen, not to anticipate the root of the next diad (Ex. 6.10).

6.10

Example 6.11 shows various other diads with their possible roots and available tones.

6.11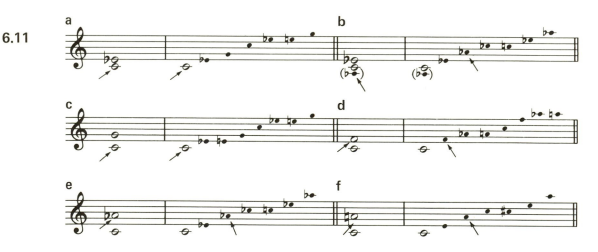

This completes the roster of diads without tension which might appear in the two-voice structure you are decorating. Any of them might be compounded, of course. A word about Example 6.11d: since the diad is P4, it would occur in the structure only under certain conditions, of which you are already aware. These same conditions would be in force if, given the diads in Example 6.11e and f, you were tempted to choose F as root. We will avoid this condition (root P4 above the bass) until we encounter it in more concrete form in Chapters 7 and 8.

If the two-voice structure embraces a diad or diads comprised of a tense interval, the procedure is not altered. The tense interval of the diad is simply added to the available chord tones and would in most cases remain the *only* tense interval available for the decoration, all other tones conforming to the principle of nontension. Care must be taken to retain the sense of resolution to the next diad tone (Ex. 6.12).

6.12

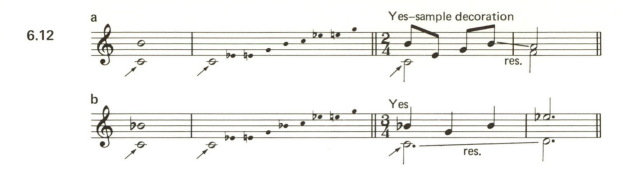

The sample decoration in Example 6.13, while melodically acceptable, does not fulfill the function called for by the original diad—to stress the D as chord tone. E♭ sounds like the chord tone. The D's sound like auxiliaries (see page 98). To render the D unequivocal, don't move *by step* to a less tense chord tone (Ex. 6.14).

6.13

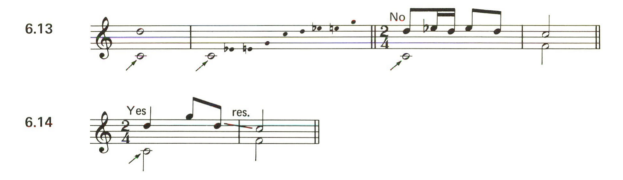

6.14

With some cases of tense diads, it may be advantageous to include among the available chord tones an additional tense interval, as in Example 6.15. In the sample decoration of this example the C in bar 1 has the strong option for downward resolution. The addition of the F♯ in the upper voice reinforces that option and therefore enhances the implication of the original diad.

6.15

If the diad is d5 or A4 (Ex. 6.16), there is, of course, no root. The choice of chord tones can be made in such a way as to keep them rootless for all practical considerations.

6.16

Or a root may be supplied (chosen) and the decorations made accordingly (Ex. 6.17a). This will again bring into play an additional tense interval. Note in this example that in the two-voice-structure diad the E is the member of A4 which is resolved—downward. The chosen root confirms the urgency of the downward resolution.

Note also that the sample decoration in Example 6.17b does not actually resolve the Bb by motion to the C, since the resolution of d5 is *inward*—to the A in the second bar.

In Example 6.17c, notice that the D and F, resulting from the choice of Bb as root, both form tense intervals with the E, but both reinforce the legitimate upward resolution of the E as prescribed by the two-voice-structure diads.

This principle applies to other tense diads as well. Since all tense intervals in the structure must be immediately resolved, at least one of the tones will move to the next diad by step, as in Example 6.17d. If the upper tone is to be resolved, then any chosen root must maintain the tension of that tone and require its resolution. If the lower tone is to be resolved, then its condition as the tense tone may or may not be retained.

6.17

Did you notice that in each of the sample decorations in Example 6.17, the first and last tone in the bar is the original diad tone? This is not mandatory, but it is a good device for making sure that the implications of a tense interval in the two-voice structure are honored. To be sure, the original diad tone is to be the stressed tone, but there are other ways of accomplishing this, as you learned in Chapter 4. Example 6.18* shows three such ways.

6.18

Other ways of decorating the upper tone of d5 and A4 will present themselves to you in context. The principles illustrated in Examples 6.16 to 6.18 should be your guide.

Voice Leading

As you make your decorations, you will need to exercise caution as you progress from one bar to the next. Be guided by the same rules which governed the progression from one diad to the next in making the two-voice structure. Example 6.19 shows six sample violations of those rules.

6.19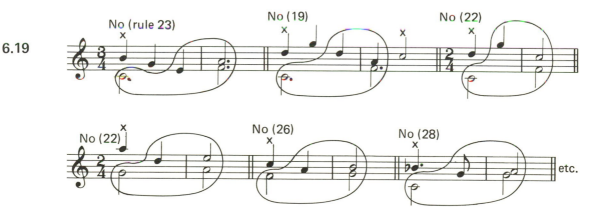

The sample melody in Example 6.20 is in keeping with the discussion up to this point, using only stable vertical intervals, except in cases of tense diads in the two-voice structure (and breaking none of the rules just mentioned!).

*In this and the following examples, the original diad tone is marked with an "X."

6.20

> Choose one of the two-voice structures you made while you were studying Chapter 5, or make a new one. Decorate the upper voice twice, using stable chord tones only, except in those cases where the two-voice-structure diad is unstable. Use contrasting styles for the two melodies. (Before making your first decorations, you might wish to review the suggestions under the heading "Making Your Melody" in Chapter 4.)

Auxiliary Tones (1)

While your melodies may be good and acceptable, like the one in Example 6.20, you may find that they sound just a bit matter-of-fact—lacking a certain harmonic, rhythmic, and expressive richness. This matter-of-factness may result from their being deprived of the melodic grace which auxiliary tones can provide.

Auxiliary tones are nonchord tones which are attached in some way to the chord tones. They are of several kinds: neighboring tones, passing tones, suspensions, appoggiaturas, anticipations, échappées (unresolved neighboring tones), cambiatas (unprepared neighboring tones), and free tones.

The Neighboring Tone

The *neighboring tone* moves by step or half-step away from a chord tone to its neighbor, then returns immediately to the same chord tone (Ex. 6.21).*

---

*Please note that this and the following examples of auxiliary tones sometimes show tones that are auxiliary to tones which form tense intervals. This is, of course, necessary because some of the two-voice-structure diads may be tense intervals. (The following abbreviations are used in the examples: N—neighboring tone; P—passing tone; S—suspension; A—appoggiatura; Ant.—anticipation; E—échappée; C—cambiata; Ch.—changing tone; F—free tone.)

6.21

Two facts regarding the neighboring tone should be noted:

1. While it *more often* occurs on the weak part of a beat or measure, it *may* appear anywhere.
2. Like all auxiliary tones, it is most effective when it forms, with the tone in the other voice, an interval of greater tension than the one formed by its "parent" chord tone. In Example 6.21a to e, for instance, the second vertical interval—the interval formed by the neighboring tone—reveals greater tension than the first and third intervals. This greater tension accomplishes two purposes:
   a. it retains the unequivocal identity of the chord tone as such;
   b. it propels the neighboring tone forward to the next tone.

In Example 6.21f to h, the neighboring tone creates tension equal to or less than that of the parent chord tone. This situation may sometimes be desirable for rhythmic or motivic reasons in the melody you are making, although, of course, it sacrifices the second of the above purposes (b). In order to retain the first of these purposes (a), the neighboring tone should be comparatively short, as is the case in Examples 6.21f to h.

If the neighboring tone is notably greater in tension than its parent chord tone, it *may* be correspondingly longer in duration (Ex. 6.22). The two chord tones flanking a neighboring tone need not be members of the same chord or diad (Ex. 6.23).

6.22

6.23

The Passing Tone

The *passing tone* (Ex. 6.24) is a little like the neighboring tone. It too moves away from a chord tone by step (always a whole- or half-step). But instead of returning to the original chord tone, it passes on *by step in the same direction* to *another* chord tone.

Like the neighboring tone also, it usually occurs on a weak part of the beat or measure, but *may* appear anywhere. And again like the neighboring tone, it is most effective if it forms a more tense interval with the other voice than the tones which flank it, but this is not nearly as important as with the neighboring tone, nor is it always feasible.

6.24

Note: In Example 6.24d, the C♯, like the B and the D, forms a C-rooted interval with the lower voice. The tension is greater, however, since it forms, in addition to its sonic tension, an augmented interval with its attendant ambiguity.

There may be more than one passing tone between the two chord tones, as in Example 6.25, and the two chord tones flanking a passing tone or group of passing tones need not be members of the same chord (Ex. 6.26).

6.25

6.26

Example 6.27 shows a decorated upper voice using stable chord tones, a neighboring tone, and several passing tones.

6.27

Again, decorate twice the upper voice of the structure you used in the exercise on page 98. This time, use stable chord tones, and neighboring and passing tones. The two melodies should be in contrast to each other.

The Suspension

The *suspension* (Ex. 6.28) is probably the most useful of all the auxiliary tones, because of its high potential for lending rhythmic, harmonic, and melodic enrichment —hence expressivity—to a melody. The suspension spans the progression from one chord, or diad, to the next, and consists of three parts:

1. *The preparation*—a chord-tone member of the first chord; the chord tone is held over (*suspended*) into the second chord.
2. *The suspension proper*—the held-over former chord tone (it should *not* be a chord tone in the second chord). The suspension is usually not longer in duration than the preparation, and it invariably appears on the strong part of the bar or the beat—most often the first beat of the second bar. The suspension should usually produce greater tension than the preparation does, and always more than the resolution. (Notice that M6 or m6 has more tension than P5, since it is farther to the right in Ex. 2.3.)
3. *The resolution*—just that. It resolves the tension of the suspension downward or upward by *step* to a chord tone in the new chord.

6.28

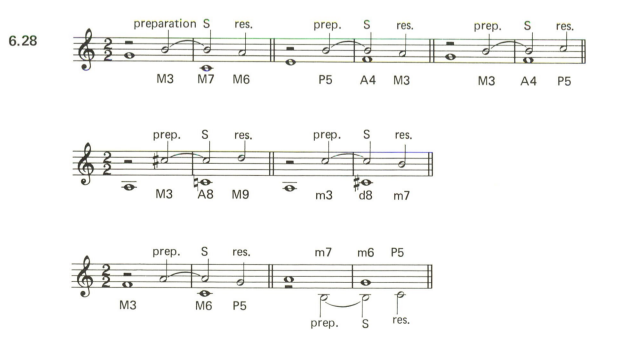

The preparation need not be the upper diad tone itself, but any chord tone as previously defined (Ex. 6.29). The same is true of the resolution. Obviously the suspension cannot be introduced unless a chord tone is available for stepwise resolution (Ex. 6.30).

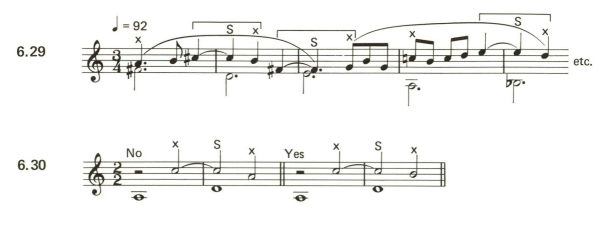

6.29

6.30

Caution: You will recall from Chapter 2 that tense intervals do not resolve to octaves or unisons. *One exception:* If it is absolutely unavoidable, 9 may resolve to 8 if the prevailing direction of the voices is in contrary motion, as in Example 6.31.

6.31

Example 6.32 shows an upper voice decoration using suspensions.

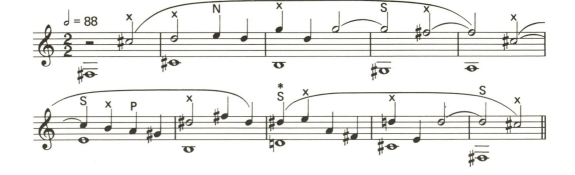

6.32

*Note that the suspension need not be tied to its preparation, but may be restruck at the moment of suspension, as here.

Using the same structure of the last two exercises, make two melodies, adding the
suspension to your melodic resources.

The Appoggiatura

The *appoggiatura* is nothing more or less than a suspension without the preparation. If
you will reexamine Examples 6.28, 6.29, and 6.31, blocking out the entire bar preceding
the suspension, you will be looking at perfectly good examples of appoggiaturas. Of
course, the appoggiatura need not be a member of the preceding chord.

They may be attacked head-on immediately in the first beat of the first bar of your
decoration, if you like. In a melodic context, however, the appoggiatura is approached by
skip—usually, but not necessarily, from the opposite direction in which it will resolve
(Ex. 6.33).

6.33

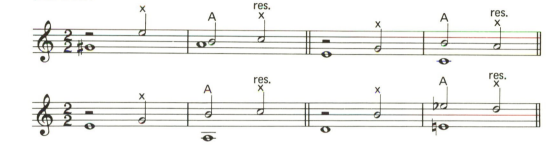

Notice that if the appoggiatura were to be approached by step it would lose its pungent
character, becoming merely an accented passing tone or neighboring tone. Like the suspension, the appoggiatura appears on a stronger part of the beat or measure than its
resolution does, and should display more intervalic tension than does its resolution.

Still using the same structure, make two upper-voice decorations including
appoggiaturas.

The Anticipation

The *anticipation* (Ex. 6.34) merely anticipates the next tone by sounding just before
it. It occurs just before a strong beat, and is most commonly used for cadential emphasis
and motivic development. Like other auxiliary tones, it is most effective if it forms a
tense interval with the other voice, and is not tied to the tone it anticipates.

6.34

The anticipation may anticipate another auxiliary tone, such as the appoggiatura (Ex. 6.35). While the anticipation is usually shorter than the surrounding tones, it can effectively be quite long if all tonal functions are clear and the tension is high—at a strong cadence, for instance (Ex. 6.36).

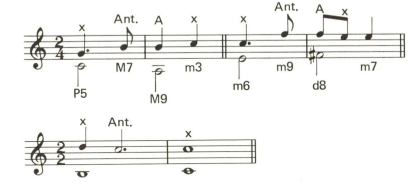

6.35

6.36

> Look over the eight decorations you have already made. Ascertain those places where the anticipation could be effective and insert it.

By now, having made a number of melodies using chord and auxiliary tones, you should be fairly adept in the art of making good and attractive melodies which are also perfectly clear in their harmonic implications and in the functions of their auxiliary tones. Relying on that security, we will now proceed to the remaining three kinds of auxiliaries. Since these three lack either resolution or preparation or both, they are just a bit more tricky to handle than those you have used up to this point. That is, they are not as closely allied with adjacent chord tones, and so there is greater danger of losing the sense of root delineation.

The Échappée

The *unresolved neighboring tone* (traditionally known as the *échappée,* or "escape tone") moves away from a chord tone *by step,* like the normal neighboring tone. Then, unlike the normal neighbor, it *skips* to another chord tone (Ex. 6.37).

6.37

The Cambiata

The *unprepared neighboring tone* (traditionally known as the *cambiata*) is the opposite, or reverse, of the échappée. Unlike the normal neighboring tone, it *skips* to a nonchord tone, and then, like the normal neighbor, resolves *by step* to a chord tone (Ex. 6.38). Note that the cambiata always occurs on a weak part of the bar or the beat. If it were to appear on the strong part, it would be an appoggiatura.

6.38

Like other auxiliary tones, the échappée and the cambiata are most effective if they form, with the other voice, greater tension than the chord tones which flank them. If they do not do this, they should be notably short in order to avoid possible root ambiguity.

Look for places in your melodies which might technically and *tastefully* accommodate an échappée or a cambiata. Insert them there. Don't be too generous with them. (Save all these melodies, by the way. You may be able to use some of them when you begin decorating the lower voice.)

Auxiliary Tones in Combination

The échappée and cambiata are often useful in combination with each other or with other auxiliary tones:

1. An échappée often skips to a cambiata. Remember that both should be tense if possible. This double usage is called the *changing tone* or *double neighboring tone* (Ex. 6.39).

6.39

2. The échappée may skip to an appoggiatura (Ex. 6.40).

6.40

3. The cambiata may be used to decorate the resolution of a suspension or an appoggiatura (Ex. 6.41).

6.41

4. The échappée may even leave a suspension or an appoggiatura by step and then proceed by skip to the resolution of the suspension or the appoggiatura. The resolution may also be decorated by a cambiata (Ex. 6.42).

6.42

The possibilities are almost endless, and you should make some melodies that experiment with the lengths to which this kind of double-auxiliary usage can be pushed—always maintaining as your *first* goal, as usual, a beautiful melody which adheres stalwartly to the tonal implications of the original two-voice structure.

Make an upper-voice decoration which uses the changing tone and one or two of the other combinations illustrated in this discussion. Remember that it is a *melody* and no mere exercise. Therefore, you may need to do two melodies in order to encompass the possibilities.

The Free Tone

The *free tone* is the last of the auxiliary tones to be examined, and it will probably be the one least often used. It is called a free tone because it is *neither* prepared *nor* resolved, nor does it serve a harmonic prupose, being always a nonchord tone. Rather, it might be used for the sake of carrying out the development of a melodic motive or to propel a meaningful step-progression. Example 6.43 is a melody decorating the upper voice, with free tones included. Note how the two free tones carry the step-progression from the F♯ in bar 6 to the final C♯.

6.43

Unstable Chord Tones

We now go on to upper-voice decorations using, as chord tones, not only the tones which form stable intervals with the given (or chosen) root, but those forming unstable or tense intervals as well.

In Example 6.44, all the tones form, with the C, intervals whose root is C (the given root), and are therefore available as chord tones. Compare this example with Example 6.8. Note that in Example 6.44 m9 and M9 are available because the root (C in this case) is the lower tone. M2 and m2 are *not* available because the upper tone would be the root (D or Db in this case), and the root of the diad would thus be disturbed.

6.44

Example 6.45 gives the available tones if A is chosen as root.

6.45

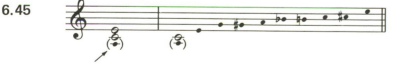

One caution: While A is in truth the root of all intervals formed by the tones shown, some of them (G and Bb, for instance) form more stable intervals if sounding with C as they will be doing when you decorate the upper voice. Then the danger of disturbing or replacing the A root is ever present. So you will want to minimize the impact of those C-rooted intervals by making them comparatively short, by placing them in inconspicuous metric positions, or by relating them immediately to the chosen diad-root by means of strong melodic skips or leading-tone progressions, as in Example 6.46.

6.46

> Now return to Examples 6.11 to 6.17, which show only the *stable* tones in each case. Rewrite each of these to include *all* available tones. Then transpose each of the intervals to two or three different pitch levels, and again write out all the available tones.

Example 6.47 shows a decoration using both stable and unstable chord tones. Compare it with Example 6.20.

(U—unstable; S—stable)

6.47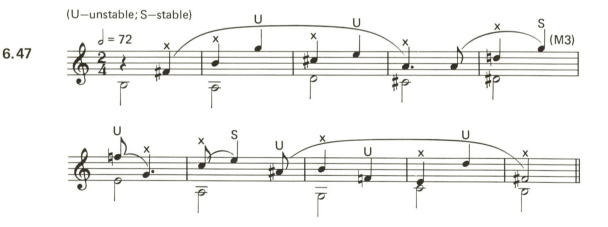

In making decorations which include unstable tones, take care to make them *sound* as chord tones rather than as auxiliaries to other, more stable, chord tones. All the identified auxiliary tones in Example 6.48 are in fact among the available chord tones in each case. But they *function* as auxiliaries because they all resolve to *more stable* intervals having the same root.

6.48

The way to ensure chord-tone function is to skip to and away from the unstable chord tone, or to resolve it to a legitimate chord tone in the next bar. In Example 6.49, all tones again are available chord tones, but this time they function as such (see also Ex. 6.13 and 6.14).

6.49

> Select another of the two-voice structures you made while studying Chapter 5, or make a new one if you prefer. In either case, it should have a comparatively weak tonal center.
>
> Decorate the upper voice twice using stable and unstable chord tones. Continue to observe the same voice-leading principles as heretofore, except that rules 19, 23, and 26 can be disregarded when unstable chord tones are used—provided the diad tones are adequately stressed.

Auxiliary Tones (2)

In addition to lending melodic flexibility, the function of auxiliary tones is to create tension. By the inclusion of the unstable intervals as chord tones, the general level of tension has been increased beyond that of the decorations which used only stable chord tones. Therefore, *some* of the value attached to auxiliary tones has been usurped. However, there is still ample validity for their use. They can still serve melodic flexibility and can still contribute to the general level of tension desired. The same principles of tension and release are in force, but at a higher saturation level of intervalic tension.

Look again at Examples 6.27 and 6.43, and you will see that in a context of stable chord tones only, some of the auxiliaries might also be unstable chord tones. The prevailing stable sound gives the function of an auxiliary to all but the stable chord tones.

There is no need to go through the auxiliaries again one by one, as Examples 6.21 to 6.43 include auxiliaries to tense tones as well as stable tones. Just remember that, on principle, the auxiliary has greater tension than the chord tone to which it resolves, whether the tone of resolution is stable or unstable.

Example 6.50 shows a melody which uses both stable and unstable chord tones with auxiliaries. Roots are indicated by the arrows.

Note that there are only five *genuine* auxiliaries—those which cannot be mistaken for chord tones—in Example 6.50. The "auxiliaries" in parentheses only sound as such in that, while they fulfill the tension-release functions of auxiliaries, they are related to the indicated roots as chord tones. This fact suggests how the use of tense chord tones foments a tension of functional ambiguity as well as simple intervalic tension.

6.50

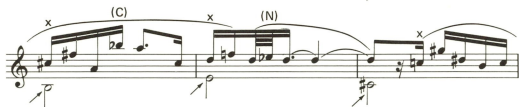

> Make several upper-voice decorations of your weak-tonic structure, using both stable and unstable chord tones, with a generous sprinkling of auxiliaries. The aim is always, of course, to make melodies which, in addition to being technically precise, speak in some way as expressive communication. They should be as beautiful and purposefully direct as it is possible for you to make them.

DECORATING THE LOWER VOICE

Look over the work you have done in decorating the upper voices of your two-voice structures. Next, you will make other melodies to go with them by decorating each of the lower voices. Strive always for a melody in the lower voice which is just as good in every way as the one already present in the upper voice.

The same melodic principles apply to the lower voice as to the upper. The same chord and auxiliary tones are available in the same ways in each bar. It would be wise to begin by making the lower melodies as simple as possible, with a minimum of decoration. They might gradually become more elaborate as you gain experience, though beauty rather than complication as such is always the aim.

So in your first efforts you should allow the existing upper-voice melody to carry the burden of musical utterance, relegating the lower one to a supporting role only. Reexamine Example 6.2 as an illustration of this kind of balance between the two melodies.

Harmonic Integrity

In decorating the upper voice, we went to some pains to make sure that the root in each measure was scrupulously delineated as each diad was decorated. Thus, each bar expressed a harmonic unit, or chord. Of course, in decorating the lower voice, that chord will be clearly retained in each measure by adhering to the same chord tones which formed the harmonic basis of the upper-voice decoration.

The upper-voice decoration in Example 6.51a delineates a comparatively simple chord —C, E, G, B♭. Thus it is easy to differentiate between chord-tone and auxiliary functions. In Example 6.51b, the situation is quite different in that the upper-voice decoration treats as a chord tone almost every tone which forms, with C, a C-rooted interval—either stable or tense. Thus the chord- and auxiliary-tone functions are not defined quite so unequivocally. You will notice in Example 6.51c that B♮ functions as a chord tone in the upper voice and as an auxiliary tone in the lower.

6.51

Voice Leading

Even as you seek to make your lower melody equal in quality, if not in complexity, to your upper one, you will find other considerations which must be taken into account. One of these is voice leading. You have already dealt with this technical and musical matter as you made second voices to go with models in forming the two-voice structure and in decorating the upper voice.

Every time the two voices move simultaneously as you make your second melody, the same voice-leading principles cited on page 75 and amended on page 97 apply.

Crossing of voices can sometimes be done if the two melodies are so well differentiated from each other rhythmically and motivically, as in Example 6.52, that identity is ensured.

6.52

When in the course of the decoration you use tense tones—either chord tones or unresolved auxiliary tones such as the échappée—you may or may not decide to give them at least a "quasi," or delayed, resolution. You can do this by letting them become parts of an ongoing step-progression, by allowing a tone to join others of its pitch as a holding tone, or by eventually resolving them after the intervention of other tones.

In Example 6.53, the high B is a tense chord tone which finds eventual resolution in the high A one bar later, also joining the ongoing step-progression. Of course, it could be left hanging, prolonging the tension, as in Example 6.54. The holding-tone procedure can be seen in the treatment of the tense chord tone E♮ in Example 6.55.

6.53
6.54

6.55

Early in this chapter you read that two melodies were "partners" in musical expression, and that they must accommodate themselves to each other in such ways as harmony, range, motive, rhythm, phrase, and texture. We have thus far covered only the first—harmony. But all these means of mutual accommodation are closely interlocked, and we can touch on the others briefly with the most pertinent guiding principles.

Range

Here I wish merely to plead that while you are making the two-voice structure which is to be decorated, you will leave enough room between the two voices for melodic maneuvers. How much room you will need depends largely on the character of the melodies you intend to compose through the decorations. A sedate melody will need hardly any, while one that moves around a great deal may prefer to have an octave, more or less, of buffer area in which it is in no danger of nudging its partner. In any case, remember that your melodies, at least the early ones, are intended to be sung by you and your fellow students.

Motive

In Chapter 4 you learned to make your melodies by exploiting in each case a very few motives—two or three. The motivic construction of the lower melody will follow the same principle. All, some, or none of the motives may be common to both melodies. The two melodies may be dependent on each other in this respect, or they may be quite individualistic. Study Examples 6.2 to 6.7 as well as the duos listed at the end of this chapter.

Rhythm

While rhythm and motive are by no means one and the same thing, they are inextricably bound to each other. This becomes evident when we subject a motive to variation without destroying its instant recognizability. Rhythm is usually the strongest identifying factor. Thus, when we were considering motives in Chapter 4 we were also speaking about rhythm. And when we studied the contrast between the motives in the Bartók melody, we meant mostly *rhythmic* contrast. At least some of the motives of your second melodies might very well be contrasted rhythmically with those of your first.

In Example 6.55, for instance, the two melodies actually share no motives. Thus, in this particular rhythmic aspect each goes its own way quite independently, even while cooperating nicely in pulse, meter, harmony, range, phrase, lyric texture, etc. Such independence can lend to the whole a kind of subtle tension—almost as though the two melodies were flirting with two different tonal centers. Perhaps they are leaning toward two different *rhythmic* centers!

   Example 6.56 is quite different in this respect. Each of the two melodies employs two rhythmic motives, but one of those motives (marked by solid brackets) is shared between them; it passes first from the upper melody to the lower, then back again in the second bar, only to be subjected to variation in the last half of bar 2 in the lower melody. Notice also how the first motive in the lower melody (marked by dashed brackets), repeated in the beginning of its second bar, contributes its ♩♩♩ to the variation of motive 2, upper melody, when that motive is repeated in the second half of bar 2, upper melody. These borrowings produce a kind of genial give-and-take between the two melodies, which flow along quite differently from those in Example 6.55.

6.56

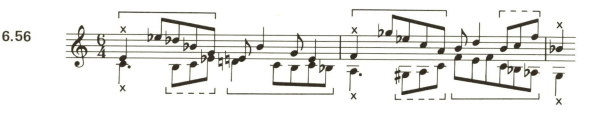

   Now look again at Example 6.55 for another facet of rhythm—asymmetrical placement of rhythmic motives. While the whole of the upper melody constitutes one complete phrase, its division by motive is irregular. The first motive—a quarter note followed by a string of even eighth notes—consumes the first 4½ beats. The second—with the syncopation ♩ ♪|♪—consumes two beats, but is immediately repeated with an extension of the last two eighths. These asymmetries could be expressed by barring the phrase as in Example 6.57.

6.57

   The lower melody of Example 6.55 exhibits no such irregularity for the most part. Rather, it joins the regular (one per bar) harmonic changes to define clearly the first and strongest beat of the 3/4 meter in which the example is cast. In this way, a rhythmic dichotomy is set up between the two melodies—the lower marking the constant three-beat pulse against which the asymmetries of the upper are all the more effective in this instance. Nevertheless, the lower melody does contain one rhythmic shift: the pair of eighths on the third beat in bars 1 and 2 occurs one beat later in its last appearance. Attention is drawn to this shift by the step-progression from F in bar 1 to E♭ in bar 4, by the strength of the appoggiatura (the same E♭) in the latter spot, and by the inter-valic contraction.

   Don't completely overlook the pair of eighths in the upper melody, bar 3, beat 3. Aurally, this pair serves as a surrogate for the two earlier pairs in the lower melody, and its placement *just there* draws further attention to the displaced pair in the lower melody, bar 4.

Example 6.56 is far more symmetrical. First of all, because of the rhythmic near-identity of the two full bars, the phrase tends to divide into two subphrases. The two full bars in each melody are rhythmically identical except for the addition of an eighth note in the second bar in each case. In the upper melody this eighth is crucial, because it provides the only asymmetry in the example—the first subphrase comes to a momentary halt at bar 1, beat 6, while the additional eighth renders the second subphrase one beat longer by carrying it over to the first beat of the next (incomplete) measure. Thus we have one six-beat and one seven-beat unit.

One further rhythmic observation: After the first beat in Example 6.55, thanks to just enough rhythmic contrast between the motives, a new note is struck in one voice or the other on every beat and half-beat—all the way through. This, of course, is not mandatory and could eventually lead to dullness. But be careful to avoid meaningless or embarrassing rhythmic halts. Pauses in which no new note is struck can be most welcome, especially if they occur with regularity or logically placed irregularity. Example 6.56 uses a pause at the beginning of each bar to set off the new harmonic unit and the symmetry of the motivic treatment.

Rhythm is sometimes asserted to be the most instinctive of our musical faculties. Perhaps this is true, but all too often that instinct is allowed to languish on a shockingly primitive level of perception. A high rhythmic art consists, at least in part, in the capacity to lend credence and conviction to the unexpected—the surprising—against the securely predictable backdrop of the even pulse. Think of rhythm not so much as a mere twitter of notes arranged in arbitrary durations, but as a purposeful utilization of time.

Phrase

You will do well to review the discussion in the "Phrase" section of Chapter 4. When you were making melodies with models as guidelines, you were obliged to take the phrase into account, at least to some extent. Now, because we are concerned with the effect of two combined melodies, the phrase takes on more significance. The reason is that in addition to the function of the phrase end as a harmonic and contoural "breath mark," the phrase itself assumes more value as a rhythmic unit. For if two (or more) melodies come simultaneously to a resting point even temporarily, that pause attracts more notice than would either melody coming singly to rest.

This property of the phrase end—or cadence—equips the composer with a very powerful tool for controlling the rhythmic flow of his piece. For instance, a duo consisting of short equal phrases—all of them cadencing simultaneously in the two melodies—might tend to produce a somewhat choppy effect (not necessarily undesirable at times), as in Example 6.58.

Perhaps the composer should make sure that each little succeeding phrase adds some new, even though minute, interest if he hopes to carry the listener along with him! (Ex. 6.59). Or the phrases could still be short and equal in length, but with those of one melody overlapping those of the other. Or they might be unequal in length, but cadence simultaneously. Or unequal phrases might overlap. The possibilities are limited only by the imagination and ingenuity of the composer. For the present, that's you. Experiment!

6.58

6.59

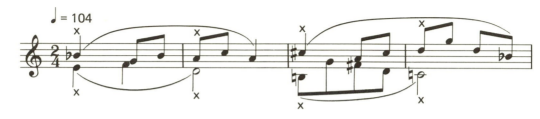

> Try some two-voice decorations with the phrases varied in the ways suggested in the above paragraph.
>
> *One caution*: Make sure that your temporary phrase cadences do not require your presence to point them out to your fellow students and your instructor. They should be self-evident. You can most readily ensure this by making certain that you have allowed ample time at cadences to take a new breath. Repeatedly sing them yourself before you bring them to class—just to make sure.

Texture

When there are only two melodies to be sung together, the question of texture might be a foregone conclusion—it is a two-voice texture. But there are matters left uncovered by that description.

Is the predominating sound the open kind produced by perfect intervals, the reasonably relaxed kind which accompanies the prominent use of the relatively stable M3, m6, m3, and M6, or the kind fraught with intervals of tension? And if the last is the case, what kind of sound produces the lion's share of that tension—M2 (and inversions), m2 (and inversions), or some combination of these? Admittedly, in two voices these factors cannot be controlled with precision. Emphasis can be controlled to a considerable extent, however.

Are the two melodies intervallically close together in range, or are the intervals between them quite large? This factor makes an appreciable difference in the sound.

Are there always new notes sounding, or does the duo rely heavily on sustained sound? Are there many notes, or are they sparsely placed? If in general they are sparsely placed, do little spates of notes erupt periodically?

Again—imagination and ingenuity!

In Examples 6.60 to 6.66, lower-voice decorations have been added to the upper-voice decorations already shown in this chapter.

Note the sparse decoration of the lower voice in Example 6.60. Since any more would seem inappropriate, only three tones are added by decoration. The lower-voice decoration in Example 6.61 is more elaborate because the slower tempo and the more elaborate upper voice can accommodate it.

In Example 6.63, note the increased activity in the lower voice in bars 4 and 9. In bar 4, the purpose is to use the lower voice to bridge the cadence. In bar 9, the purpose is precadential rhythmic tension.

There is no more decoration in the lower voice of Example 6.64 than in Example 6.62, again because of the relatively self-sufficient upper voice. Notice the complementary rhythmic, motivic, and phrase structure of the two voices.

In Example 6.65, the upper voice is, of course, constructed with the use of stable and unstable chord tones plus auxiliaries. This raises the level of tension and at the same time contributes to the incipient tonal instability. In the decoration of this lower voice, these facts have to be borne in mind. The tones employed are therefore equally tense, in the interest of stylistic consistency.

6.60

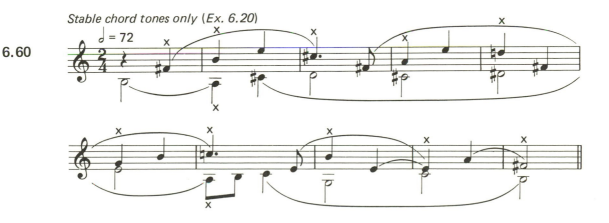

Stable chord tones, neighboring and passing tones (Ex. 6.27)

6.61

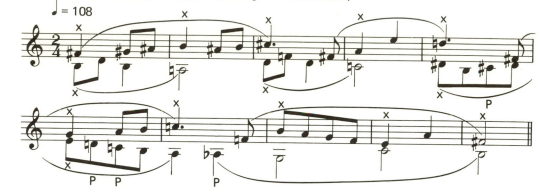

With suspensions (Ex. 6.32)

6.62

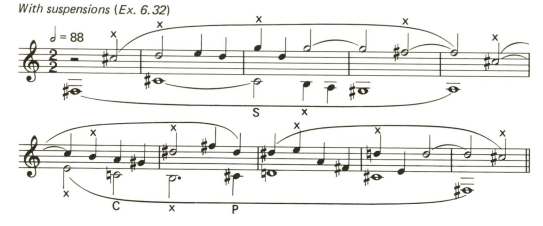

With free tones (Ex. 6.43)

6.63

Stable and unstable chord tones (6.47)

6.64

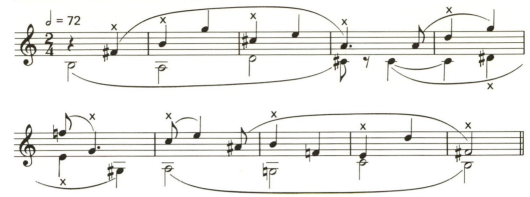

Stable and unstable chord tones, plus auxiliaries (Ex. 6.50)

6.65

Analyze all the decorated two-voice structures given in this chapter (Ex. 6.2 to 6.7 and 6.58 to 6.65). First determine the root in each bar. Then determine the tension displayed by each of the chord tones, stable or unstable, and number these tensions according to the table on page 82.

Lastly, mark all the auxiliary tones with the proper letter (for example, N—neighbor, P—passing tone).

Etc.

''Etc.''—the last of the ways in which the two melodies should accommodate each other —is not, of course, a musical term. Perhaps it seems rather vague. It's not, really. But it is very broad in what it encompasses. For it is meant to include all those myriad instances, large and small, where aesthetic judgment is called on. Such instances, by their very nature, are not answerable to any rules or even to any suggestions. What sorts (plural, please note) of melodies will contrast characteristically with another without danger of overwhelming it? When do you curtail the activity of one in order to allow momentary play to the other? How do you do this without leaving mutilating scars on the melody momentarily curtailed? How do you produce the maximum effect with a minimum of notes? How do you decide when and in what manner one melody may imitate the other with fresh effect and to a positive end rather than with a negative or obvious result?

Strictly technical matters are, of course, inviolate, but the above questions and many others will always demand your best judgment, both now and as you accumulate experience. That is the meaning of the word *technique* in its higher sense—the overlay of purposefully motivated judgment on mechanical considerations. There is only one way to acquire at least the foundation for understanding this technique, and through it a deeper penetration of the meaning of the art: court it assiduously. Bring to every little duo all the skill you can muster. But when it is sung in class, don't be satisfied if your fellow students and instructor merely note that it is good, or technically accurate, or even interesting. Try to move them. That's the last etc.!

Now decorate the lower voices of your already upper-voice-decorated two-voice structures. Then make new two-voice structures and decorate first the lower voice and then the upper. The technique is the same, though it may not be quite as easy to accommodate a new upper melody to an already existing lower melody, since the former—just by its upper placement—tends to steal the show.

Begin with two-voice structures which display a strong tonic, then employ every means at your disposal to weaken—even obliterate—the tonal center. Let the decorations conform to the style of the two-voice structure.

SUGGESTED DUOS FOR STUDY

As you are engaged in this enterprise of writing the best possible little duos, you should also be taking time between efforts to examine pieces that have been written by composers in the recent as well as the more distant past. Here is a short list to get you started. The Bach, Bartók, and Etler pieces are small. Work on them first. You or your instructor will find, or already know of, others whose perusal will be equally profitable to you.

> J. S. Bach: Two-Part Inventions
> Béla Bartók: Forty-four Duets for Violins
> Alvin Etler: Duo for Oboe and Viola
> Michael Haydn: Fourteen Easy Duets (for violins)
> Paul Hindemith: Piece for Bassoon and Cello
> Darius Milhaud: Duo for Two Violins
>   Sonata for Two Violins
> Wallingford Riegger: Variations for Violin and Viola
> Adolph Weiss: Sonata for Flute and Viola

Perhaps life would be just a little easier for you if I were to include a full-blown analysis of some of these, as I did with the melodies in Chapter 4. However, you now have at your fingertips enough knowledge to do this yourself—with greater profit for your pains—with the help of your instructor.

In doing this, apply all the yardsticks that we have discussed up to this point—phrase, motive, form, tonal centers, root sequence, functional support, tension, and stability of root determinant—and all the rest of the technical and aesthetic factors that have gradually been seeping into your musical consciousness.

Remember that the work you have been doing has been rather clinical—distilled for concentration on one technique and then another. Any composer whose piece you may analyze probably uses somewhat different applications of the principles which have informed our work. But the same principles are there. You have only to look for them.

7

THE THREE-VOICE STRUCTURE

It is axiomatic that if a half-dozen tones sound at the same time, they produce a richer sonority than one tone sounding by itself. But a melody written to sound all by itself enjoys far more room for maneuver than one which must take into account the activity and "space" requirements of one, two, three, four (or even more) other melodies. Thus, it can be said that the greater the number of voices, the greater is the music's dependence on sonorities and their interaction for its effect. Conversely, the fewer the voices, the greater can—and usually must—be the concentration on linear interest.

In the polarity between one and many voices, the nodal point is three-voice writing. Three simultaneous tones are usually enough to satisfy considerably more than the ear's minimum sonority requirements, and none of the voices need be unduly cramped for maneuvering space. Once you have mastered the combining of three voices, you need learn little more—mostly limitations on the techniques you already know—in order to use four or more voices. Rare indeed are those musical passages with even three, not to say four, voices of equal linear interest. Far more commonly the texture consists of a two-voice "outer skin" with one or more inner voices whose minimal melodic interest makes no pretense of masking their main function—filler.

COMBINING THE THREE VOICES

We will unabashedly bear these concepts in mind as we enter on our three-voice efforts. In the beginning, you should place the third voice in the middle of the texture. First make a model. Place a second voice above it, as in Chapter 5. Take care to leave room between them for the insertion of a middle voice. Construct the middle, or third, voice. When your skill in these two procedures is reasonably secure, add a third voice on the top, and then a third voice on the bottom. Finally you will be constructing six different three-voice structures on each model:

second	model	third	second	third	model
third	third	second	model	model	second
model	second	model	third	second	third

I repeat: When you make the second voice, always leave room for the third, if it is between the first and second, and always make sure that the third voice is in a singable range, if it is above or below the other two. Often the model will have to be transposed to another pitch level in order to accomplish this. If the third voice is to be between the other two, try at first, in making the second voice, to use no vertical interval smaller than a fifth—to be approached and left by contrary motion. As your skill in handling doublings and tension increases, smaller distances may be possible at times.

In the interest of vocal identity it is even more important here than in the two-voice structure to avoid crossing the voices. Independence of voices is likewise served, as before, by the avoidance of coincidental linear climaxes. A sharper ear and eye will be required here than in Chapter 5, since there may be as many as six such climaxes. Should there truly be no way to avoid such a coincidence, take care that it is not between the *outer* climaxes.

Melodic Contour

The third voice, like the model and the second voice before it, should strive for the best possible melodic contour. However, since it must adapt itself to *two* voices already present and unchangeable, it cannot even approach the same flexibility as the other two. The third voice then is subject to the same rules as the model—with five exceptions:

    I. The first and last tones need not be identical unless the third voice is the lower one.

    2. The last tone may be approached by any melodically permissible progression.

    3. Any tone may be repeated, with or without intervening tones. (*Note:* An *upper* climax tone may be repeated in the third voice, only if done without intervening tones.)

    4. The direction need not change after four tones in the same direction.

    5. Scalar passages of more than three tones are permissible.

The first two of these exceptions are, of course, identical with the first two which applied to the second voice (see page 71). As was the case with that voice, these two do not appreciably alter the melodic contour. Exceptions 3, 4, and 5 do, and are to be invoked with great care. If the third voice is in the middle, the repeated tones and scalar passages can be a positive asset to the three-voice structure, possibly adding a smoother dimension to the tripartite voice leading. However, if that voice is one of the outer lines, care must be taken so that the application of any of the last three exceptions will not devitalize the linear contour—particularly if the third voice is the upper one. But all will not be lost if the upper voice must be shot through with repeated tones and scalar passages. They may represent the lesser of two (or more) evils; they may even present special challenges when you attempt to restore interest through melodic decoration in the next chapter.

Chords and Roots

The materials available for combining the three voices are essentially the same as for the two-voice structure—all intervals and any combination of tones. *Chord* will be the term applied to any simultaneous combination of three tones. *Caution:* Any chord *may* embrace up to three tense intervals. All tensions must be immediately resolved. Example 7.1a gives some instances of chords requiring no resolution. Example 7.1b illustrates chords with one, two, and three tense intervals. The resolution shown for each—to a chord without tension—is, of course, not the only one.

7.1

It is pertinent to remind you here that resolution is defined as the motion of a voice to *less* tension, not necessarily to *no* tension, and that the unresolved tone of a tense interval may move to a tone forming either a stable interval or another tense one (see Ex. 7.2a). Example 7.2b shows each of the chords of Example 7.1b, but this time with most of the tensions resolved to other tensions, which in turn require resolution in whatever chord may follow.

7.2

Any three-note chord will contain three intervals. In most cases one of those intervals will be a more stable one (to the left in Ex. 2.3) than the other two. The root of the most stable interval will dominate as root of the whole chord as well (Ex. 7.3).

7.3

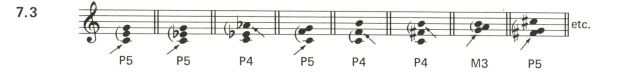

If two of the intervals in a chord are equally stable, then the lower of their two roots will function as root of the chord (Ex. 7.4). Two interval-roots of comparable strength may, between them, create ambiguity as to the root of the chord. P5 is by far the more stable interval in Example 7.5, but C is root of *two* intervals and is registrally lower. Context could resolve the ambiguity to a degree, but registral redistribution of the same notes would eliminate it, as in Example 7.6.

In still other cases (Ex. 7.7) no interval is sufficiently stable to win in combat over the others, except possibly in context. Again, registral changes could partially, though never wholly, resolve these ambiguities through bestowal on one of the tones the authority of isolation in the bass, as in Example 7.8. You may sometimes find these ambiguities useful, especially if you are aiming at a weak tonal center or a wide "elastic" stretch in the middle of the structure.

Since the function of the cadence is to supply a sense of finality, the root of the last chord should be in the bottom voice. This chord will most often be devoid of tension but should contain, at the most, no more tension than the chord or chords immediately preceding it (Ex. 7.9).

7.9

A covered octave or unison is permitted at the cadence provided its upper member is not approached by an upward leap. The tone thus doubled in the final chord should be the tonic. The tonic *may* even be tripled at the cadence.

You might do well here to review the passage in Chapter 5 which seeks to ensure an unequivocally new root for each new vertical interval (page 76). The principles are the same in three voices as in two. If you have successfully accomplished this aim in your two-voice structures, then you are reasonably safe from danger in adding a third voice. However, the addition of a third voice to certain innocent-looking two-voice progressions can result in a three-voice progression in which the six tones add up to a forbidden seventh chord containing a tritone.

Example 7.10 shows first such an innocent-looking two-voice progression, then the third-voice pitfall, and, finally, ten alternate choices for the third voice—some ''farther out'' than others, but all acceptable in proper context. Perhaps there are more. You will notice that in all of them the third voice moves stepwise, since only as a last resort would all the voices skip.

7.10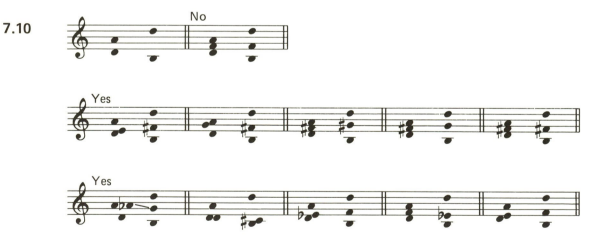

Voice Leading

In the interest of sonic consistency and smooth chord progressions, certain rules of simple voice leading are mandatory. Explanations hardly seem necessary, for you are already aware of the effects such rules seek to achieve or prevent:

1. Except in the last chord, never double a tone at either the octave or the unison if it is at all avoidable. If such a doubling is truly unavoidable, some notes are more advantageously doubled than others:
   a. the tonic, the fifth above the tonic (dominant), and the fifth below the tonic (subdominant)
   b. the root of a chord—(a) and (b) might coincide
2. Avoid doubling any active tone, such as:
   a. the active member of any tense interval (that is, the tone you have chosen to resolve)
   b. any tone functioning as a leading tone

An active tone, by definition, demands action—resolution. When two tones (a doubled active tone) demand identical resolution, they carry the implication of that action, whether or not they actually proceed by parallel unisons or octaves.

The outer voices may *not* skip simultaneously in the same direction, though the middle voice *may* skip simultaneously in the same direction with either of the outer voices.

But: In all progressions, at least one voice should move by step *if at all possible.* Progressions containing two stepwise voices are even smoother. If all voices *must* move by skip, then it is particularly important to avoid doubling in either chord of the progression.

Covered perfect fifths and fourths in which the upper voice skips upward may be used between any but the outside voices provided that neither chord contains a doubled tone. (Other covered fourths and fifths present no problems anywhere.)

Parallel perfect intervals are to be avoided except for stepwise parallel fourths between the two upper voices when no doubling is present in either chord.

No tone of the lower voice should ever be immediately anticipated *in the same octave* by a tone of the middle voice.

In only two circumstances should you use any chord whose root is a perfect fourth above the bass note:

1. When the bass moves through it stepwise without a change of direction (Ex. 7.11a)
2. When the bass remains stationary (Ex. 7.11b)

7.11

Caution: When P4 is already present in the two-voice structure, and when the lower voice does *not* move through that P4 stepwise, then the tone which you use in the third voice *must* be one which will either make the lower tone of the P4 the root or assume that function itself (Ex. 7.12a).

Note: The P4 in Example 7.12a is a compound interval. If it were a simple interval in the two-voice structure, then a third voice could not be placed between them (Ex. 7.12b).

The augmented unison and the augmented or diminished octave are handled exactly as in the two-voice structure (see page 81).

7.12

CONTROL OF THE TONIC

The chapters on the model and on the two-voice structure closed with discussions of the technical and aesthetic possibilities available in each case. This chapter will do the same. Tonic- and tension-control options increased appreciably with the addition of the second voice to the model. With the addition of a third voice, they burgeon forth in profusion.

First, the matter of tonal stability. I think little need be added here regarding the three factors which contribute to tonic strength or weakness: roots that are closely or distantly related to the tonic, placement of the chords containing those roots, and the relative stability of the intervals which determine them. Of course, in adding a third voice to the two-voice structure you are limited by linear considerations. Even so, there are often a number of possibilities in the choice of each tone. This choice can either confirm the tonal organization already present, weaken it, or alter it drastically—most probably it will strike somewhere between the extremes of the first and second possibilities.

As an example, let us suppose the two-voice structure contains a reasonably noncommittal M6 with root A: . Here are the possibilities when a third voice is added:

1. It can strengthen the root by the addition of another, stronger, interval of which A is also the root (Ex. 7.13a).
2. It can confirm the root without appreciably strengthening it (Ex. 7.13b).

3. It can challenge the root by setting up a multiplicity of possible roots (Ex. 7.13c). (Some of these are more ambiguous than others and much depends on context.)

4. It can destroy the root by adding another identical interval (m3 or M6); in this case the result would also be the addition of the very wobbly tritone (Ex. 7.13d).

5. Or it can change the root altogether by turning the C into the root or by substituting another tone as root (Ex. 7.13e).

7.13

We have thus added to our original A and C, unchangeable as part of the two-voice structure, each of the remaining ten tones, each in three different octaves. Each of the thirty possibilities is different from all the others in sonority, and in some cases the root delineation is at least potentially altered by registral change. Of course, only a few of these possibilities will be open to you in any given situation, but your choice will in each case be governed by at least two considerations—on the one hand linear grace and function, and on the other hand the tonal function of the resultant three-tone chord.

At times the possibilities for altering the root of a two-voice-structure diad will be severely limited. For instance, if the interval given in the two-voice structure should be P5, then there is only one way to change the root: by adding another P5 below it (Ex. 7.14). Even this does not lend great strength to the new root, C, since chords made of equal intervals can seldom have strong roots. Two strong fifths are two *conflicting* fifths, and the lower root has the advantage only of register over the upper one.

7.14

If, however, the given diad is an unstable interval, there are numerous possibilities for imbuing the chord with a stronger root. Consider the extreme case of d5 (Ex. 7.15).

7.15

Remember, then, that the more stable the diad, the more limited are the possibilities for root substitution, and the more tense the diad, the greater the number of possible root substitutions. Therefore, a two-voice structure with many stable intervals offers little possibility for manipulating the tonal organization by means of the third voice.

For instance, the two-voice structure in Example 7.16 is one in which stable intervals predominate (seven out of nine). Note the roots and their tonal functions. The root-determining intervals are given between the staves.

7.16

Tension	2	0	0	0	1	0	0	0	1	0 = Total 2
		m3	M3	P5	m7	m3	M6	P5	m7	M3
Roots	F	Eb	D	E	A	E	Bb	C	F
Functions	T			L		L	S	D	T = Total 6

Neither of the added third voices illustrated in Example 7.17a and b alters the root structure appreciably, with only two changes in (a) and a single questionable one in (b).

7.17

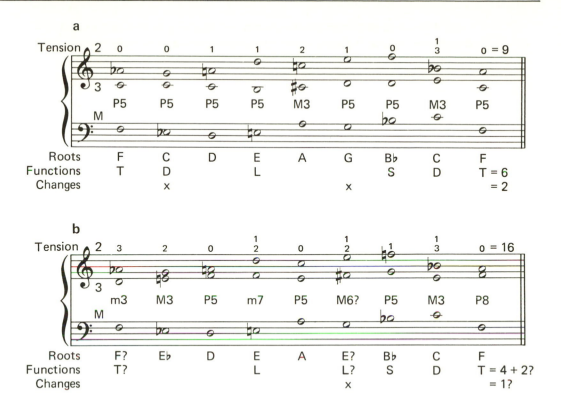

CONTROL OF TENSION

Root-Determining Intervals

Examples 7.16 and 7.17 should show that, with an abundance of stable intervals in the two-voice setting, the addition of a third voice will usually effect very little change in the tonal center and its support. Few of the diad roots are apt to be altered. The functions of dominant, subdominant, and leading tones will scarcely be affected in their contribution to the stability of the tonic. The greatest tonal contrast as such between these three structures occurs in the root-determining intervals. Note that Example 7.17a, with P5 for seven of its nine root-determining intervals, has a tension total of only 9, while Example 7.17b, with only three perfect fifths and a variety of *somewhat* less stable intervals, gathers together a tension total of 16—an increase of a little over 77 percent. The differences between the two in the stability of their root-determining intervals and the aggregate amount of tension are important factors contributing to the very strong, not to say obvious, tonic confirmation in (a) as against the somewhat more subtle one in (b). Also contributing to this contrast is the *placement* of tension: (a) has four chords entirely devoid of tension, whose roots are T, D, S, and T in that order; (b) has three such tensionless chords, but their roots include no functional tones other than the final tonic. The unequivocally stable momentary impression given the ear by tensionless chords in a context of greater tension cannot fail to affect the hearer's sense of tonal balance. It should be added, however, that none of these three structures is in the slightest danger of actually "losing" its tonic. The number of functional roots as well as the placement of S, D, and T at the very end and in the habitually strongest order gives that assurance. Notice that the tension is greatest in the penultimate chord.

In contrast to Example 7.16, look at the two-voice structure in Example 7.18. There is tension in six of its ten diads, including the final one, for a tension total of 8—as against 2 in Example 7.16. Like the structure in Example 7.16, this one is in no danger of losing its tonic. Indeed, it displays one more functional root, with S, D, and T similarly placed at the cadence. The tonal center is, however, rendered a little less obvious by the absence of the stronger root-determining intervals M3, P4, and P5; the presence of four inverted and two diminished intervals; the somewhat ambiguous parallel major ninths; and the mildly tense final interval.

7.18

Because of the greater two-voice tension and the less stable diads, the addition of the third voices in Example 7.19 effects considerably more root changes and a rather startling increase in tension over the two structures of Example 7.17a and b. The tonic is somewhat weakened in Example 7.19a and b by the small decrease in functional roots, but even more by the loss of the dominant and a clear subdominant in the penultimate and antepenultimate chords—with an ambiguous root change from A to G in (b). Notice that the root determinants remain predominantly less stable than in Examples 7.16 and 7.17.

7.19

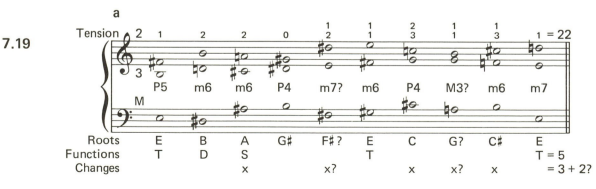

Strategic Placement of Tension

In the last few examples, the tension has been handled so that it occurs at strategic places: in Examples 7.18 and 7.19a at the upper climax of the lower voice (tension totals 2 and 5 respectively), and in the penultimate chord of 7.19a (total 4), but in 7.19b at the outside climaxes and in the penultimate chord. This use of tension to point up climaxes is the opposite of that in 7.17a and b, since in 7.17a the upper climax is devoid of tension, while in 7.17b the lower climax is tensionless. Both usages—adding or dropping tension at climaxes—are perfectly valid, since focus is the purpose in both cases. It is quite coincidental that the greatest tension in Example 7.17a and b falls on the upper climax of the lower voice. The real function of *that* concentration of tension is cadential.

Example 7.20 consists of five additional three-voice structures built on the model used in Example 7.17a. These five, together with Example 7.17a itself, constitute one model worked out in the six different distributions outlined on page 122. This model is one of

7.20

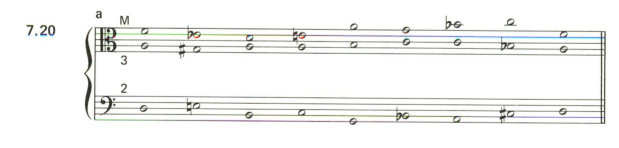

7.20

those with a strong tonal center by virtue of the placement of functional tones, particularly at the cadence. Nevertheless, you will notice that the root relationships do change, sometimes rather drastically, from one structure to the next. Analyze each of them carefully in the manner used in Examples 7.16 to 7.19. Play them all repeatedly to savor the effect each produces in its individual deployment of functions and tensions.

Example 7.21 consists of six more three-voice structures. Unlike the previous group, each is built on a model whose tonal center has only minimal support. Play and analyze each of these structures exactly as you did in the previous group.

In Example 7.21a, compare the amount of functional support (five out of nine chords) with that in Example 7.20a (seven out of nine). Then compare its functional strength (two T, one D, and two L) with that of Example 7.20a (three T, two D, one S, and one L). Then compare the number of those functions which are ambiguous in root delineation (one in Ex. 7.20a, three in Ex. 7.21a). Do you see the reasons why the tonal center is weak here—in addition to the ambiguity already implicit in the model?

In Example 7.21b, note that the final tonic is itself ambiguous, to say the least. Notice also the adjacent F roots in chords 7 and 8. When the root sequence is as noncommittal as it is here, the appearance of two fresh tones in chord 8 is enough to give a sense of motion. Example 7.21c also has an ambiguous final tonic, and only three perfect intervals as root determinants—and those functionally unrelated to the "tonic."

Throughout Example 7.21 I hope you have noticed the occasionally unorthodox resolutions of tense intervals. (And did you notice the one in Ex. 7.17b? In Chapter 9 we will discuss the use of a considerable number of such resolutions.)

When you have noted all roots, the intervals which determine them, and all the tensions in Example 7.21, then compare the result of your analysis with that of Example 7.20. Pay particular attention to the amount and placement of functional support for the tonal center, the comparative stability of the intervals which determine all roots, and the amount and placement of tension.

7.21

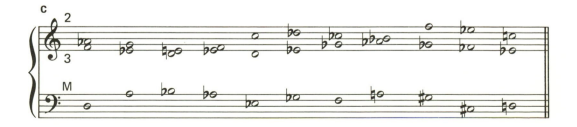

7.21

> You are now ready to start making three-voice structures of your own. Begin by
> using models with strong tonics. When these structures are free of mistakes, use
> progressively weaker tonics, fewer functional roots, less stable root determinants,
> and a greater amount of tension. As you are engaged in this work, never forget that
> the primary aim is music. Strive for the graceful horizontal line, chords that sound
> attractive besides serving a structural end, and purposeful control of tension.

Prevailing Sound

The discussion of tension must include one other factor. It is not only possible, but
perhaps regrettably easy, to compose a three-voice structure in which the tensions are
very well placed and expertly handled in all respects but one. In pushing your skills to the
last measure, try to achieve (in addition to everything else!) a basic *prevailing sound*.

During the period of traditional harmonic practice, for example, the prevailing sound
was supplied almost exclusively by the ubiquitous major and minor thirds. Any deviation

from this sound, such as the addition of a seventh, a ninth, or even an auxiliary tone, was sparingly employed, usually for clearly recognizable formal purposes such as cadential emphasis or a convincing modulation from one key to another. Herein lies one of the secrets of the enormous vitality of this music—the establishment of *norms,* from which the composer could depart in order to control and call attention to some formal or expressive feature.

In learning to drive home your own musical points, always try to establish your own prevailing sound as a norm. It might help you to think of this sound in terms of a particular prevailing tension level—expressed in terms of the tension digits 0, 1, 2, and 3 we have used in this chapter. From this prevailing level, whether low or high, you can depart either upward or downward as your formal or expressive needs of the moment require. Try writing a few structures with this concept in mind.

ABOUT BREAKING THE RULES

I hesitate to write the following paragraphs. They have to do with the fallibility of the rules given in Chapters 5 and 7. There is sure to be a time when the function of one or another of these rules is simply not convincing to you. This is the time for some careful ear- and soul-searching! Is your momentary rejection of its veracity merely the result of established musical habit which may or may not be relevant to the specific situation? Does following the rule in this particular case actually fail to accomplish what it is supposed to do? Does breaking the rule in this particular case really disrupt the aims and purposes of the two- or three-voice structure? (Ex. 7.17b and 7.19b each contain such a calculated breach, as do one or two others. Did you spot them?)

Regardless of your answers to these questions, from time to time your misgivings could very well be justified. If you are honestly convinced that they are, then go ahead and disregard the rule, make a note of it, and subject the result to the scrutiny of your peers and your instructor. But resort to this only after exhaustive efforts to do the job strictly within the confines of the rules. More often than not such efforts will result in good and valuable musical solutions which otherwise you could never have tucked away among your musical resources. Such efforts will thus sharpen your musical wits and immeasurably expand the scope of your musical imagination even when they fail in the end to produce the best of all possible progressions.

Scientists have been known to speak appreciatively of the numberless failures on which may depend the eventual successful solution of a research problem. Are we musicians any more immune to the rigors of experiment? Perhaps the commitment of even the average scientist to life on the frontiers of knowledge, in contrast to the typical musician's commitment to life within the frontiers of Notre Dame, Leipzig, Esterhazy, Mannheim, Vienna, Bayreuth, or even Nashville, may at least partially explain the ascendancy of the sciences over the arts in the priorities of today's materialistic culture!

But when the rare time comes when no amount of effort can find the way, at least seek to live up to the spirit of the law if not the letter. Possibly there are choices to be made between two minor evils. Make the choice and then *listen.* Maybe you can find a still better way. . . .

8 THREE MELODIES

We now turn to the decoration of the voices in the three-voice structure. The aim is the composition of three melodies which support and either balance or complement one another. As in Chapters 4 and 6, the tones of each voice serve as the stress guideline for each of the melodies. Each chord of the three-voice structure will occupy one measure.

While the skills to be developed in combining three melodies are perhaps more exacting than those required in combining two, the techniques are precisely the same in principle. They differ only in some details. Start by decorating the upper line, then the lower line, and finally the middle line. When you have acquired some skill in this sequence, you should then decorate the voices in different sequences, starting with the lower or middle voice. The problems in each case will be somewhat different, since the second and third voices to be decorated will have to accommodate the voice already decorated without overwhelming it.

Caution: Take care not to fill each melody with so much activity that the three obscure one another with too many conflicting simultaneous demands on the ear. Remember that the ear tends to focus on one thing only at any given moment. This is not to say that two of the three melodies must be reduced to mere accompaniment, but only that it is part of the composer's job to be constantly aware of where he is riveting the ear's attention at every step along the way.

CHORD TONES

In the three-voice structure, of course, each vertical unit is a three-note chord (triad) rather than a two-note interval (diad). No matter what they are, these three tones are to be considered chord tones and are to be afforded the same stresses we gave the model tones and the diad tones in Chapters 3 and 5. This means that in many more instances than in two-voice decoration *all* the chord tones you need will already be present. It also means that in all but a very few cases the root of each triad will be unequivocal. Tones other than the triad members may be treated as chord tones, if they adhere to the root of that triad (see Ex. 6.8).

If the root of any triad is so ambiguous as to exert no influence as root, then you are at liberty to perpetuate that ambiguity by using, in the manner of chord tones, whatever additional tones do no violence to the context—that is, tones which do not bring about disturbing redundancies with the tones of the adjoining triads.

AUXILIARY TONES

All the auxiliaries listed in Chapter 6 are, of course, available for use in any of the three melodies. The principle of greater tension in the auxiliary than in its parent tone is the same, of course, as in two voices, except that in three voices there are always two other tones, rather than only one, with which the auxiliary may form that tension. In Example 8.1a, the neighboring tone G♯ forms its greater tension with the G♮ in the middle voice. In Example 8.1b, the neighboring tone forms its greater tension with the C of the lower voice. In each case the tension caused by the neighboring tone is 2 as against 1 for the original triad. Be careful when adding the decoration of one voice to that of another that you do not negate the effect of the auxiliaries used in the decoration of the first.

8.1

In Example 8.2a to e, the tension level of the parent triad is 0. In (a), the appoggiatura takes its effect from the tension it forms with the C in the lower voice. In (b), the double appoggiatura is poor because that tension has been removed by doubling the B. In (c) and (d), the double appoggiaturas are valid because the condition of greater tension than the parent chord is still present. And even the triple appoggiatura in (e) retains its punch and justification for the same reason. The three auxiliaries need not be resolved, of course, at the same time (Ex. 8.3).

The essential conditions in the use of auxiliaries are always that the triad retain its recognizable integrity as three chord tones, and that the auxiliaries fulfill their function by virtue of greater recognizable tension. While only the appoggiatura has been used here as illustration, these conditions apply equally to all auxiliaries.

8.2

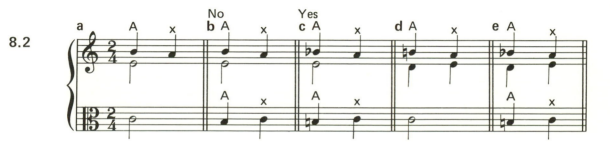

8.3

VOICE LEADING

Having made numberless two- and three-voice structures and decorated many of the two-voice ones, you should by now know what good voice leading is. Nothing further technically will be said, for the principles are exactly the same in three-voice as in two-voice decoration, and are always in force. (Review what was said in Chapter 6 under this same heading.)

In your writing of models, second and third voices, and decorations, you have been continually admonished to make melodies which are not just technically adequate, but graceful and beautiful as well. Try to remember that voice leading can also be graceful in addition to being merely functional. Take care as a matter of course that there are no technical faults in your voice leading but, beyond that, never put down a note unless there is something about its placement in pitch and time which tickles your fancy and pleases your ear.

It was pointed out earlier that while the undecorated three-voice structure should offer all the positive values present in the two-voice structure, it offers the additional factor of reasonably full sonority. The same is generally true of decorated two- and three-voice structures. When only two melodies are heard simultaneously, there can never be any sound consisting of more than two tones. Harmonic sonority, then, is a matter of only minimal interest, with most of the interest and the delight perforce derived from the characteristic qualities of the two melodies themselves and from their mutual interplay.

DECORATING THE THREE-VOICE STRUCTURE

In writing three simultaneous melodies you should strive to regale the ear with that same kind of interest and delight. But never overlook the availability of fuller sonority, and learn to couple it with those other manifestations of melodic compatibility. In fact, except for momentary rests, every moment throughout every one of your three-voice decorations will reveal some kind of three-tone sonority. Each and every one of these moments deserves a good and attractive sound! This sound is not guaranteed to your decorations no matter how good, rich, well planned, and purposeful the sonorities were in the original three-voice structure. It can be guaranteed only by your constant awareness of all sounds you put to paper and submit to the ear.

Models with Strong Tonics

Example 8.4a to f shows six samples of decorated three-voice structures. The structures decorated are those in Examples 7.17a and 7.20a to e. Most of them are transposed to accommodate normal vocal ranges, though some of the decorations are more instrumental than vocal in character. Remember that all those structures were based on a model with very strong functional support for the tonic. Remember too that in spite of that built-in tonic power, the addition of the second and third voices has confirmed that tonic in some of the structures, while in others the tonic has been weakened to a degree.

In each of the decorations, the type of musical idea seeks to reinforce the harmonic style of the three-voice structure. For instance, Examples 8.4a and b are in a melodic style which bears some resemblance to sixteenth-century polyphony, while Example 8.4c is quite romantic in style.

Example 8.4a is purely vocal in concept, and it is suggested not only that you study it, but that the whole class sing it as well—not that it would be ineffective if played on various instruments. Only suspensions and neighboring tones are used in this barely minimal decoration—so minimal that motives can hardly be said to exist.

8.4

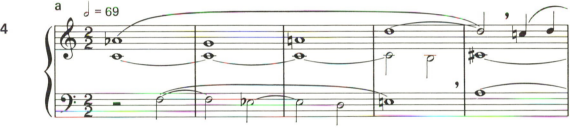

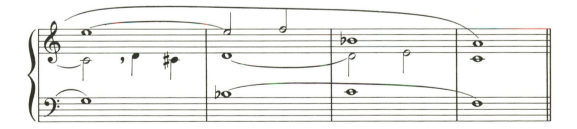

Example 8.4b is in the same vocal style as its predecessor. The resolutions of all the suspensions are decorated with unprepared neighboring tones; these contribute a motive all their own. Notice in the sixth bar, top voice, how that motive is extended through the use of the passing tone D (fourth quarter) to inaugurate the running quarters which

continue in the middle voice nearly to the end. This produces a cumulative rhythmic effect coinciding with the increase of tension which marks the seventh and eighth bars. Notice also the introduction of the root-disturbing A♭ in bar 7. This, in addition to the "surprise" attendant to the new note, increases the tension in a chord which was already somewhat ambiguous as to its root foundation.

8.4

Example 8.4c could be sung, but its sound is intended to be that of violin, viola, and cello—with the cello playing the middle voice. The lower voice is here written in the viola clef to facilitate your performing it this way if you have players available. As for the shifting meter: it was mentioned earlier, in the discussion of two-voice decorations, that the bars need not be equal in length. In this decoration the middle voice was composed first, and the bar lengths were ordered to suit that melody. Notice how that melody exploits just two motives. The first appears in bars 1, 3, 5, and 8, the second in bars 2, 4, 7, 8, and 9. Neither is ever repeated identically. The variation is slight enough to ensure continuity of thought—just enough of a change so that a new dimension, however minimal, is added each time it returns.

The upper voice, with its upbeat opening to echo that of the middle voice just two beats earlier, is slow to enter the proceedings—shortening its durations (A♭, 7 beats; B♭, 4 beats; and finally D♭, 1½ beats) until it is drawn into sharing the second motive with the middle voice. The only appreciable rhythmic motion in the lower voice occurs when there is a temporary cessation of activity in the two upper voices.

Note the restruck suspension in the middle voice from bar 3 to bar 4. Except for the échappée and the free tone, every kind of auxiliary is used, including combinations of more than one. In bar 1 the E anticipates the appoggiatura in the next bar. Similarly, the F♯ in bar 6 anticipates a similar appoggiatura. A♮ in bar 7 is a cambiata, though the A *looks* more like a delayed chromatic passing tone between A♭ and B♭.

8.4

Example 8.4d is not meant to be sung. Write it out for such instruments as are available in class, preferably woodwinds. In its use of motives with minute variations, the example should be virtually self-explanatory. There is one free tone—the C in bar 6, middle voice.

It is there for two reasons: to maintain the rhythmic figure (𝅘𝅥 𝅘𝅥𝅮 𝅘𝅥𝅮 𝅘𝅥) which has already occurred in bars 2 and 4, top voice; and to maintain the step-progression which began with the first note in the top voice (E-E♭-D-the C in question-B♭). One chord is altered through the decoration—bar 3, from B♭ root to G root. A touch of humor is intended in the sixteenth-note figures, whose interval span increases consistently from m2 in bar 2, through M2 (bar 3), and m3 (bars 4 and 5), to P4 in bar 6—only to be loquaciously flattened out again in the next to the last bar and rhythmically reined in.

Strings could play Example 8.4e—or winds. During its first five bars, except for suspensions and one passing tone, all tones are chord tones—many of them tense ones, of course. In the third bar the suspended B♭ produces less tension than the original chord (F, A, G). This is rectified at the earliest possible moment by the C in the upper voice, which restores the tension in the suspension and at the same time confirms the original root, F. In the sixth bar, notice the restriking of the suspended F♯ before resolution. The original root in bar 7—D—is not a strong one, hence the liberty (page 139) of perpetuating the ambiguity by the introduction of the A♭, which tends to change the root to E. But immediately, at the end of the bar, with the sound of the A, the root D is confirmed and made stronger than it was in the first place. This strengthening is by careful design, for if you will look back at the original three-voice structure (Ex. 7.20d), you will see that the bottom tone of the final chord lacks root authority. This strengthening is another liberty taken for aesthetic reasons. The strength of the strong dominant seventh chord (with good tension level) in the penultimate bar, coupled with the strong tonic root just preceding it, confirms the tonal center adequately.

8.4

Have fun analyzing Example 8.4f! In making the three-voice structure, it became evident that the best solution entailed a triple tonic at the beginning and end. This sound, together with the repeated tonic in the third (lower) voice, suggested the possibility of retaining the presence of that tonic in every bar. This kind of holding tone—a chord tone held through one or more intervening chords until it again becomes a member of a sub-sequent chord—is called an *organ point.* The organ point, as it is added to all the chords, produces a higher level of tension—not only in the immediate intervalic relationships, but also psychologically for the listener as he measures each of the intervening chords against the constantly held or repeated tone. In this example the organ point is, in almost every case, also handled as one of the eight types of auxiliary tones listed in Chapter 6. Can you find the ones which are *not* so treated?

Look at the eighth bar. The chord is D♭, B, G—root G. The last two beats of the top voice constitute an anticipation, but one which is interrupted by the insertion of a repe-tition of the chord tone G. If the G♯ in the middle voice were not so short and if it did not sound simultaneously with the G in the upper voice, it would change the root to D♭, but that is open to subjective interpretation, since the root G of the original chord is a little ambiguous at best, countered as it is by the lower registral position of the D♭—that D♭ being also the root of the m7 D♭-B! The question is academic, since in either case the propulsion to the final tonic is inevitable. B is suspended to the final bar. If this were not the case and the first note, middle voice, last bar were C, then the A would merely be an unresolved neighboring tone or échappée. Since, however, the B *is* suspended, it becomes merely one of those dual auxiliaries—the resolution of the suspension decorated by the unprepared neighboring tone or cambiata, D♭.

Play, study, and analyze Example 8.4a to f thoroughly.

Models with Weak Tonics

Example 8.5 consists of decorations of the six three-voice structures from Example 7.21. All the models except the last, as well as all the structures, have weak tonal centers and the resultant minipieces sometimes deny the tonal center almost completely. Again, the melodic style of each seeks to confirm the harmonic style of the structure it decorates.

Example 8.5a is meant to be sung, and hence maintains very simple melodic lines with mostly stepwise motion and small, easy skips. The cadence, with its upward skip of a perfect fourth, is stronger in this decoration than in the five which follow. Note the preponderance of suspensions, and the tendency toward short, overlapping phrases.

In Example 8.5b, note the imitative overlapping phrases, especially between the two upper voices, and the contrasting motive used primarily in the lower voice. This should be played on woodwind instruments, but if strings are what you have, the loss is minimal.

A glance at the three-voice structure on which Example 8.5c is built (Ex. 7.21e) reveals an upper voice which is somewhat less than fascinating in its contours, primarily because of its perfectly legitimate repetitions of G, A, and B♭ (as here transposed). The decoration, to be played by woodwinds, therefore seeks to place emphasis on color by means of the all-pervading trill motive, contrasted with staccato repeated notes.

8.5

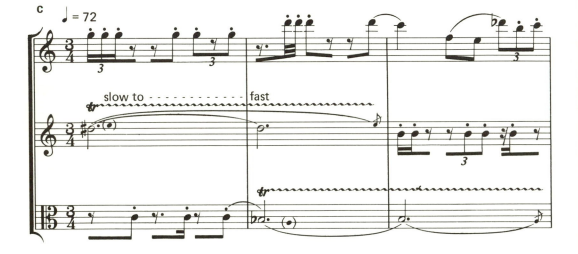

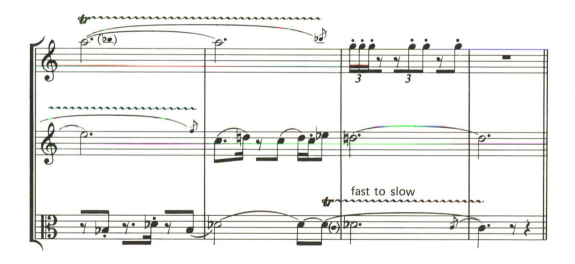

In Example 8.5d, the rhythmic contrast is expressed by two-against-three divisions of the beat—top voice, triplets; middle voice, eighth notes; lower voice, both, though they do borrow from each other. Notice that the triplets are played detached while the eighths are generally slurred. This decoration also illustrates the use of a little two-tone cell such as the one you observed in the Bartók melody in Chapter 4—Eb-D in bar 1; E-F in bar 4; Ab-G in bars 5 and 6.

d

8.5

The structure decorated in Example 8.5e (Ex. 7.21f) features a number of parallel seconds. The decoration seeks to capitalize on that sound by retaining those parallels intact. As a little compositional gambit, note that in the first phrase (bars 1 to 3) all voices move together, while in the remainder of the piece there is conflict of speed between the three parts. When you first played the structure, you may have noticed the overlap between the lower voices in the progression between chords 8 and 9, which couples with the A1 in chord 9 to create quite a marked ambiguity. Note the accent on that chord in the decoration. Also be aware of how the stepwise progressions in all voices between chords 1 and 2,

3 and 4, 6 and 7, and 8 and 9 make this kind of decoration possible within our rather limiting rules—chord 2 consisting of three neighboring tones to chord 1 and vice versa, etc.

8.5

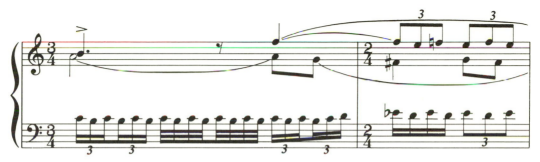

The final decoration (Ex. 8.5f) uses a simple kind of space notation, one of several means by which recent composers have sought to bring the performer into the creative process. The metronome mark indicates that the spaces between the dotted bar lines are to pass at the rate of 50 per minute. The tones indicated by the black noteheads are to sound as staccato as possible and are to divide the *time* between the bars approximately as the printed notes divide the *space* between the bars. Notes with open heads are to be held as long as the *beams* indicate. For example, since the beam covering the first three bars in the lower voice is unbroken, the first three notes are to be played legato, in one breath or bow.

8.5

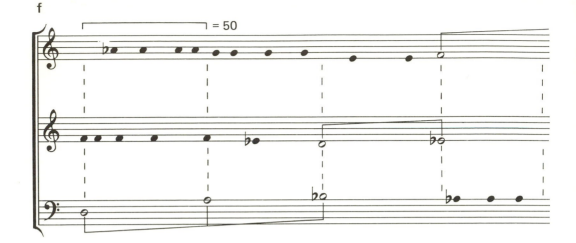

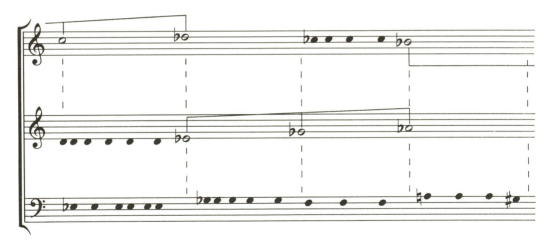

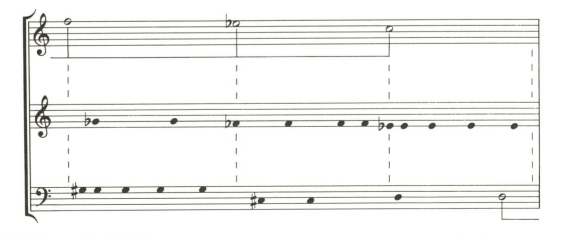

> Analyze all the decorations in Example 8.5 as you did those in Example 8.4.

The principal requirement for combining three melodies, as against combining two, is not the step-by-step assimilation of more and more knowledge. The necessary body of knowledge is not staggering in any case. But experience is something else—you need that in great quantities. So your task is to write many three-voice decorations.

Base your decorations on a variety of three-voice structures, ranging all the way from those with very obvious tonics to those with the most obscure. Let the decorations be in keeping stylistically with the structures. Generally, you should, in each decoration, pursue a specific aim similar to those revealed in the descriptions following each decoration in Examples 8.4 and 8.5. In this endeavor your progress will be measured not in assimilation of facts, but in growth of quality. That is your overall aim.

SUGGESTED TRIOS FOR STUDY

Take every opportunity to examine three-voice writings of all kinds of composers. Here is a starter list:

J. S. Bach: Three-Part Inventions
Ingolf Dahl: Concerta a tre (for clarinet, viola, and cello)
Anton Dvořák: Terzetto (for two violins and viola)
Alvin Etler: Sonata (for oboe, clarinet, and viola)
            Five Pieces (for three recorders)
            Three Pieces (for three recorders)
Orlando Gibbons: Fantasies (in three parts)
Joseph Haydn: Divertimentos 1 to 6 (for violin [flute], viola, and cello)
            Trio (for horn, viola, and cello)
Paul Hindemith: Trios for Strings, Nos. 1 and 2
W. A. Mozart: Divertimento, K. 563
Quincy Porter: Little Trio (for flute, violin, and viola)
Henry Purcell: Fantasias in 3
Arnold Schoenberg: Trio for Strings, Op. 45

9 EXTENSION OF TECHNIQUES

The work that you have done thus far, particularly that set forth in Chapters 3, 5, and 7, has been of a rather clinical nature. If at times the rules have seemed rigid to you, I hope that along the way you have come to the realization that such rigidity represents merely the quickest and most direct path toward understanding how tones relate to one another, not only by virtue of their intrinsic physical properties, but through long-established habit as well.

Every specific rule, however, is actually neither more nor less than the narrowest manifestation of some larger general principle. Most of these principles are limited to musical and technical considerations which have evolved empirically over countless generations. One such principle, for example, is the fact that two voices which parallel each other too closely tend to lose their individual identity. In making the two-voice structure we have two narrow rules which reflect this principle: no parallel perfect intervals, and no simultaneous leaps in the same direction. In addition, we seek a balance between contrary and similar motion.

There are other principles which are more broadly based, reaching at least toward, if not into, questions of psychological and aesthetic satisfaction and fulfillment. An example might be the principle of the rise and fall of tension. Our narrow rule requires the immediate resolution of each interval of tension. Within our narrow limits we also try to arrange those tensions strategically.

During the history of Western music the very broadest principles, such as those giving rise to overall formal concepts, have undergone barely perceptible change, if any at all. Presumably they are somehow so deeply embedded in the physical world, including the human sense organs, that adherence to them is all but automatic. Technical principles can change much more quickly—if any change measured in decades, generations, or centuries can be called rapid. But each era—short or long—has had its own set of specifics by means of which it has given heed to principles. Our own era is no exception, and the guiding principles distilled in our "rules" can be summarized as follows:

1. Linear grace
2. Linear independence
3. Tonal coherence
4. Tonal motion and direction (rhythm)
5. Tension control
6. Span of interest (point of departure, departure, and return—form)
7. Style (prevailing sound)

Quite understandably, principles overlap in their application and usually some kind of compromise is called for so that perfection in one of them will not inadvertently destroy the function of another. History offers a proliferation of such compromises—for example:

> Much of the linear grace typical of Gregorian chant was sacrificed to the development of polyphony.
>
> A very large measure of linear independence, not to mention grace, was sacrificed to the standardization of harmonic sequence that accompanied the development of tonality.
>
> In the nineteenth and early twentieth centuries, concepts of formal balance and symmetry had to fight hard for survival against the onslaught of personalized expression and extramusical "content," with the increasing employment of dissonance, chromaticism, and monumental performing resources.
>
> Tonal coherence, motion, and direction were placed in serious jeopardy by the development of serialistic techniques.

Even on the small scale of your own work, these checks and balances among principles have inevitably exerted a very strong force. Your second voices must sacrifice some of the linear purity of the model in the interest of tonal coherence. Your third voices must at times almost totally eschew melodic grace and linear independence in favor of overall sonority, tonal coherence, tonal motion and direction, tension control, span of interest, style, convincing voice leading, or any combination of these and other factors. Your control of tension must sometimes be sacrificed to such things as tonal coherence or span of interest. Any of these principles may at times give way at least momentarily to the greater satisfaction of another. In pursuit of your momentary aim you are often required to choose among riches, or to substitute a minor evil for a greater one.

Ideally, perhaps, no principle would ever need to be sacrificed to another and each would operate to its maximum effect, but in fact this is seldom possible, nor is it always to be desired. However, in the exercise of such controls your hand is often restrained by responsibility to the rigidity of specific rules. While Examples 7.16 to 7.21 show that a considerable amount of control is possible through resourceful manipulation within these strict limitations, extensions of the application of some of the rules can immeasurably increase your freedom of choice without seriously jeopardizing the principles they represent.

These extensions will now be spelled out for you one at a time, each with one or more examples of its use in the three-voice structure. After reading about each one and studying the examples, you should make a few three-voice structures of your own employing it. Thus each one will in turn become part of your technical resources.

EXTENDED TENSE INTERVAL RESOLUTIONS

Interrupted Resolution

The resolution of a tense interval may be interrupted by one or more intervening tones. In the three-voice structure this involves one or more intervening chords as well (Ex. 9.1a). The interrupted resolution is more effective if the intervening tone itself also requires resolution to the same tone (Ex. 9.1b).

9.1

In the construction of Example 9.2, the interrupted resolution not only enhances the interest span, but allows greater freedom in constructing the second voice; it permits reservation of the lower climax for the penultimate diad and it provides a better balance between the motions.

9.2

Delayed Resolution

The resolution of a tense interval may be delayed by repeating it one or more times before its proper resolution. The tone to be resolved should remain tense in each of its repetitions, and in each of its repetitions it should require resolution in the same direction as in its first appearance. Its eventual resolution will of course be in that direction. In Example 9.3, each of the C's requires—and finally gets—downward resolution. Obviously, this kind of resolution is possible only in the third voice, the only voice admitting repeated tones.

9.3

Focusing the tension in this way on a single tone and prolonging it until its latest possible resolution can heighten its effect immeasurably, rendering it almost unbearable even in these miniature surroundings, and doubly infusing its resolution with satisfying relief (Ex. 9.4).

9.4

The delayed resolution can be combined with the interrupted resolution, as in Example 9.5, where the little nest of cumulative tensions just before the cadence is heightened by the additional tensions of twofold suspense. The final chord, itself embracing a tense interval, is more satisfying as a result.

9.5

Note the following things in this same example:

1. The "crescendo" in degree of tension in chords 5 through 7.
2. The parallel fifths in the second progression. It is the best solution under the circumstances, and is only very rarely justified as an extension of rule 45 (parallel perfect fourths in the upper voices).
3. The sequence embodied in the first six tones of the upper voice. This sacrifice is made in the interest of cumulative tension and the avoidance of a B♮ in the top voice, third chord, prior to resolution of the B♭ in the lower voice, second chord.

The effect of the sequence can be either confirmed or minimized by means of phrase rhythm in the decoration. In Example 9.6b and c, note the variety of phrase lengths which all but obliterate the sequential effect.

9.6

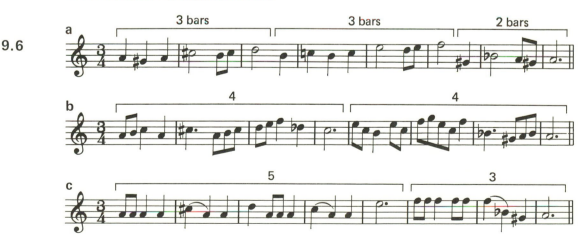

Surrogate Resolution

If a tense tone (1) skips a P4 or P5 up or down, and if the new tone (1a) then moves by step—preferably m2—in the same direction which would have resolved the original tense tone, a sense of resolution is effected (Ex. 9.7a). The stepwise motion following the skip replaces the step which would have resolved the tension normally. The condition that justifies the liberty here is in the very close relationship (P5 or P4) between tones 1 and 1a.

9.7

The surrogate resolution, like the interrupted resolution, is even more effective if tone 1a is part of a new tense interval requiring resolution—preferably by half-step—in the same direction as the original tone would have been resolved (Ex. 9.7b). Example 9.8 shows the surrogate resolution in a three-voice structure.

9.8

Deceptive Resolution

Two factors govern the resolution of a tense interval:

1. Inward or outward direction of resolution
2. Release of the tension

When a resolution fulfills the first requirement but faults on the second by proceeding to the "wrong" note, it is called a *deceptive resolution.* In the deceptive resolution itself, the tension is not usually released; this can be accomplished only by the stepwise (usually m2) resolution of the new tension *in the same voice* and *usually* in the same direction (Ex. 9.9)—sometimes with an interruption.

Without unduly belaboring a point, the m7 (chord 10) in Example 9.10 may be said to resolve in no less than three different ways:

1. Deceptively to F♯ in chord 11
2. Outwardly, with interruption, to G in chord 12
3. Normally to E in chord 13, with two interruptions

9.9

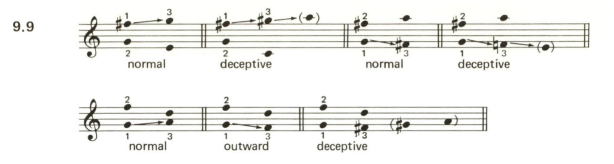

In this way the original m7 is resolved just a bit more satisfactorily each time in each of the three chords immediately following. It must be admitted that this somewhat complicated procedure is obscured to a degree by other simultaneous occurrences in Example 9.10:

1. The deceptive resolution changes direction as prescribed in Example 9.9, but instead of the normal half-step following the G♯, there is an interruption (C♯), followed by A♯ instead of the normal A. A♯ then completes the whole thing by a half-step progression to B—and final satisfaction. This produces an extension of the total resolution illustrated in Example 9.9.
2. Each tone encountered along this path (F♯, G♯, A♯) is nudged along toward that final satisfaction by a new tense interval (d3, d8, d8, respectively) requiring resolution to the next.
3. The tone which gives the original m7 its normal resolution (E, chord 13) is foiled in the attempt by the very sharp and ambiguous tension (E, E♭) of which it is a part.
4. This last comes at the exact point (chord 13) where the deceptive resolution would have ended on A if it had not been interrupted. Hence the final satisfaction is doubly postponed.

9.10

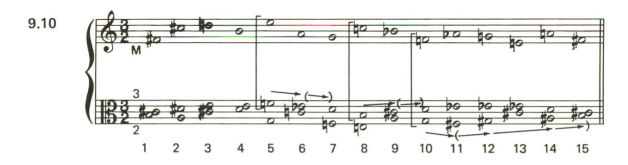

And while all of the above is going on, each of the vocal lines is in the process of regaining its original starting tone, and the overall range of two octaves is gently narrowing down, mainly through the quasi-sequential intervalic contraction in the upper voice, to the P5 with which the structure began.

Outward Resolution of m7

Under certain mitigating circumstances, particularly in constructing the third voice, m7 may resolve outward, as in Example 9.11. Unlike M7, m7 itself carries no intrinsic justification for such a resolution. Hence the outward resolution must ordinarily be dictated by some special condition or specific aim in making the three-voice structure. In Example 9.12a the momentum of the scale passage in the third voice carries us safely past the basically inferior resolution. In Example 9.12b the outward resolutions of m7 are an aid in the attempt to maintain the prevailing sounds of M2 and M3 and to place a sharper tension at the upper climax.

In the latter example, note the common root of diads 4 and 5 in the two-voice structure. This is only very rarely permissible, in the certain knowledge that the third voice will rectify the weakness by altering at least one of the roots. In this case both roots change through the addition of the third voice.

9.11

9.12

Treatment of A8 (d8, A1)

Delayed Resolution

Under favorable conditions, such as a preponderance of half-step progressions in all voices, the second member of A8 (d8, A1) may be introduced before the first member has been resolved. This effects a subtle increase and prolongation of the tension caused by the A8 (d8, A1). But it is very seldom satisfactory unless *both* members eventually achieve half-step resolution. Example 9.13 shows two augmented octaves whose resolutions are thus delayed.

9.13

Transferred Resolution

The first member of A8 (d8 or A1) may at times be transferred to another voice and be properly and normally resolved there. This practice can be risky for the well-being of tonal coherence unless the first member receives also some *other* kind of explanation. In Example 9.14a, the E in chord 2 is transferred to the upper voice, where it is immediately resolved before the E♯ appears in that same upper voice. However, the E in the middle voice is *also* given an extended and delayed resolution downward through D and C and finally by half-step to B (M2-M2-m2 instead of M2-m2). Note in addition that F♯ is the root of both the penultimate and the antepenultimate chords. The F♯ root, however—being determined by m6 as against m9 and M7—is much stronger in the penultimate chord than in the one before it, the registral factor notwithstanding. That cumulative strength is the means of justification, in keeping with a long-honored cadential principle.

Example 9.14b shows three transferred resolutions. The D in the third voice (chord 1) is transferred to *both* the other voices. Similarly, the E in the second voice (chord 2) is transferred to the upper voice for immediate resolution.

9.14

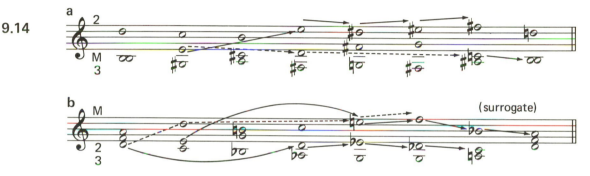

Surrogate Resolution

A8, d8, and A1 are subject to surrogate resolution just as are tense vertical intervals (Ex. 9.15). Careful now—there's a whole bevy of surrogate resolutions in this example:

1. A and A♭ (A8) would normally resolve outward. Both do so through their surrogates, E and D♭, respectively.
2. E and E♭ (d8) would normally resolve inward. E♭ does so through its surrogate, B♭, while E♭ resolves directly to F.
3. E♭ and A (d5) would normally resolve inward. Both do so through their surrogates, B♭ and E, respectively.

A total of five surrogate resolutions in the course of four chords! Things *can* get complicated.

Note in addition the three upper-voice tones in chords 5, 6, and 7—in violation of rule 6. The tension generated by that "dangling" E♭ reinforces the other tensions in this area, and its resolution by the final D contributes to the "sneeze" of the cadence. This is a further controlled liberty, taking advantage, for cadential reasons, of a formulation hitherto avoided because of its potentially disruptive quality.

9.15

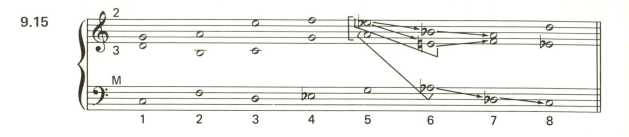

EXTENDED THIRD-VOICE TECHNIQUES

Treatment of Half-Steps

In the third voice a half-step neighboring tone to a repeated tone may appear quite independently of any previous tone (in any of the voices) with which it may form A8, d8, or A1 (Ex. 9.16). There is no need for resolution of the previous tone. Similarly, two consecutive half-steps may appear in the third voice, as in the same example. This is an especially safe procedure if the first and third tones are neighboring tones to a repeated tone. To be sure, the first G (chord 1) does get a gratuitous and much extended step-progression resolution upward (M2, M2, M2, m2). The G in chord 4 does not. Neither *requires* resolution.

Note in addition the unresolved d4 in tones 7 and 9 of the upper voice. The acceptability (and singability) of this unresolved tension is entrusted to the inevitable and rather obvious cadence. Meanwhile it makes its contribution to the span of interest.

9.16

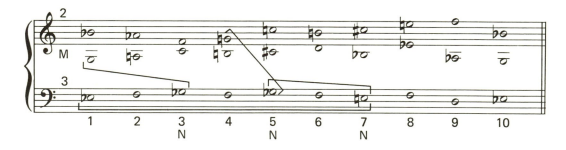

Skips of a d3

The third voice may skip a diminished third and then return a half-step in the opposite direction. The effect is similar to that of a changing tone or double neighboring tone. While d3 is functionally a third, its impact on the ear is like a whole-step—M2. Therefore, for practical purposes the two-voice progression in Example 9.17 does not constitute simultaneous leaps in the same direction.

9.17

In Example 9.18, notice the six successive F's in the top voice and how each of the six requires downward resolution. Even when it arrives, in chord 8, it has been interrupted by the D♯. The root in chord 5 is a P4 above the bass F♯—hardly disruptive, since all the attention has been directed to the tension revolving around the upper F♮.

9.18

I hope that as you proceed through these examples you are taking note of the illustrations they contain of the various types of resolutions discussed earlier in the chapter—and are using them in your own three-voice structures. Perhaps you have also observed that as technical extensions proliferate, the importance of strong roots and root sequences deteriorates in favor of fresh notes in each progression as a means of harmonic propulsion.

Further Third-Voice Expansions

Steps Beyond P5 Skip

In Example 9.19,* the third voice skips a perfect fifth and then proceeds in the same direction by step—not one step but two. This is not out of keeping with the reliance of the third voice on stepwise progressions beyond those tolerated in the model and the second voice. Furthermore, such a gesture is not apt to seem disproportionate in a structure the length of this example. Lastly, such a gesture can add welcome interest to a voice which is almost by definition more static than the other two.

9.19

*For obvious reasons, you'd best arrange to have Example 9.19 played by woodwinds or strings.

Outlined Triads

Even a directly outlined triad—especially an augmented or diminished one—is unlikely, considering the restlessness of the lines and the root structure of Example 9.19, to violate the principles which have heretofore prohibited such formulations (see chords 9 through 12, where an augmented triad is outlined).

Diminished Interval Skips

In addition to a diminished third, the third voice may also skip a diminished fourth or fifth—provided it subsequently—immediately, in most cases—honors the required inward resolution of those intervals. Tones 11 and 12 of Example 9.19 show such a skip and resolution. Note in addition the seemingly unresolved A1 in upper-voice tones 11 to 14. Actually, the principle of surrogate resolution is here extended to a single voice, G resolving through its surrogate, C, to B.

Incidentally, had you noticed that two deceptive resolutions "inadvertently" slipped into Example 9.19 (chords 4 and 8)?

SIGNIFICANCE OF TECHNICAL EXTENSIONS

I hope the discussion thus far may open up for you a conception of the significance of the various technical extensions covered in this chapter. Without these extensions—that is, as long as each interval of tension has to be resolved immediately—the effect created by tense intervals is nominally ended with the advent of the next chord. At best, tensions and their resolutions, even if they sometimes overlap, can only be strung along in tandem fashion so as to add their individual contributions to the general tonic-oriented principle of tonal coherence.

Most of the techniques discussed in this chapter have the effect of *prolonging the influence* of tense intervals. For instance, you have seen (in Ex. 9.10) how a single deceptive resolution must necessarily have a profound regulatory effect at least on the two following chords—and it usually extends its residual force a good deal further than that. One reason is that whatever auditory nerve ending is stimulated by the impact of a tense interval must remain stimulated while awaiting the soothing resolution. Another reason is that, following the deceptive resolution proper, the voice carrying that resolution is charged with unresolved tension until it attains the final satisfaction of complete release. As you have seen, that satisfaction may be postponed for some time (in Ex. 9.10 through the final third of the entire structure) by a variety of means.

Not all music, but certainly much of it that has been honored by time (say twenty years to several hundred) displays as one of its characteristics a great multiplicity of simultaneous and often conflicting strands of melodic, harmonic, rhythmic, dynamic, textural, or other motion. (Earlier you observed some of these in the step-progressions and tonal relationships embodied in the melodies studied in Chapter 4.) These strands usually move at different rates of speed, in various tonal relationships to one another, in different timbres, etc. On occasion several or even all of them may culminate in a single common goal. At other times they may aim at separate but somehow related goals.

In addition to technical competence, the quality which more than any other distinguishes among the great, the good, the fair, and the poor performer is precisely his or her perception of these strands and their musical significance, plus the ability to reveal both with clarity and aplomb. But no amount of perspicacity on the part of a performer can "reveal" anything in the music that is not there. It is the tension-bearing interaction of these strands which, more powerfully than any other single factor, engages, rivets, and commands the hearer's empathetic involvement.

You should always have in mind the realization that these three-voice structures are not the music itself, but the structural skeleton to which the flesh and blood of musical utterance eventually adheres. In this study that flesh and blood is brought to living reality through the skill—and the love—with which you infuse the decoration of each of the voices. The vocal direction and the basic linear-harmonic relationships are set by the structure. Rhythmic particulars, phrase structure, motivic character—and every other element which can contribute to the seduction of the ears, the mind, and the heart—must be supplied in the decoration. The mature composer deals directly in the stuff of these latter considerations, but the good or the great composer never loses awareness of these vital underlying strands of which you are becoming aware in making your three-voice structures. Expertly and sensitively combined, they can contribute enormously to the development of style.

PREVAILING SOUND AND STYLE

One aspect of style is the persistence of a prevailing sound. This concept was touched on earlier, but until now it has not been possible to pursue the notion.

In Example 9.20, the prevailing sound is 1 (see page 82), and while there are only two M2's as such in the structure, there are only four chords which do not contain at least one M2 in inversion (m7) or in octave transposition (M9). Thus the prevailing sound is evident. The four chords from which the tension is subtracted have roots F♯, C♯, A, and F♯. These tones provide a gentle focus on the tonic, which is not noticeably supported by the sequence of roots. To three of the chords are added tensions stronger than the prevailing 1. These are strategically placed at the two outer climaxes and in the cadential progression.

9.20

The control and placement of tension takes over the job of ensuring the formal and tonal coherence that is sometimes entrusted to the tonal orientation of root sequence, which in this structure is—of itself—somewhat less than strongly supportive of the tonal center. The combination of all these features would have been extremely difficult, if not impossible, without reliance on the technical extensions discussed in this chapter. Search them out through analysis.

In Example 9.21, the specific interval of M2 is employed at every possible opportunity. In the places where its use is not feasible, m7 or M9 is substituted. It can be said, however, that M2 really prevails, since there are no fewer than eleven of them. You should note that in those instances of parallel major seconds the progression moves by half-step to avoid its being weakened by clumsy anticipations. Note also that the M2 (A, B) in the third chord is not resolved at all. In this context no harm results, since the focus is very clearly on the specific sonority of M2, this sonority can even be enhanced by non-resolution, especially in a string of parallel progressions. Did you spot the two violations of rule 6? Analyze the structure carefully for technical extensions, tension placement, root progression, and tonic strength.

9.21

Make one or two three-voice structures, using every device at your command to arrive at a prevailing M2 sound.

The sound of Example 9.22 is quite different from that of the two preceding examples, since the prevailing sound is 2 rather than 1. To achieve this degree of sonic unity, together with the maintenance of good vocal lines, requires considerable reliance on the technical extensions covered in this chapter—and more. There are at least eight interrupted resolutions, two surrogate resolutions, a deceptive resolution, an unresolved A5, two unresolved augmented octaves, and a d4 melodic progression. In addition, the penultimate chord has its root placed "illegally" a perfect fourth above the bottom voice. This root placement is hardly disruptive in a context in which only six chords, this one among them, have a root determined by an interval more stable than m6. Thus root stability in the penultimate chord compensates for its lack of sonic gravity (see pages 80 and 127).

9.22

Now look at the root sequence in relation to tonic stability. Even in the first and last chords the lower tone can hardly be imagined as root except by authority of lower position. The real roots of these two chords are E♭ and G, respectively. Nor do the roots between these two lend any palpable support to a tonic. Not only are there very few roots which unequivocally relate to a possible E tonic, but the roots themselves are weak and sometimes controversial. We seem to be losing tonic orientation! Very well, that happened in the art at least fifty years ago.

So what is left in this structure, and in similarly oriented music, which gives it tonal form? It is evident that not all the principles relating to tonal coherence have been sacrificed:

1. The last chord has the least tension—1.
2. The two chords which constitute the cadence progression have the most stable root determinants of any chord in the structure except one (chord 8, B root).
3. Each of the three lines displays, especially in its last half-dozen notes, a convincing convergence toward its own final tone. This is particularly true of the third voice.
4. Forward propulsion is maintained from the beginning by the intervalic tensions, heightened by their prolongation through various extended resolutions, and duly alleviated at the cadence.

In the two structures shown in Examples 9.24 and 9.25, the prevailing sound is even more ubiquitous. It is not just 2, but 2 plus M3 and m3 in octave transposition (Ex. 9.23).

9.23

In Example 9.24, not only is the tension level the same in all chords, but the intervalic content of all chords, except for octave transpositions, is identical. Certain compromises had to be made in order to bring this about:

1. In the making of the second voice each diad had to be one of the three intervals of Example 9.23, which resulted in the linear use of simple triad outlines.*

2. Since these outlined triads are virtually mandatory in the circumstance, they are turned to advantage in that one of the triads outlined is the dominant (the only tonic-supporting root not present in the root sequence), while the one preceding it stands in leading-tone relationship to that dominant.

3. Consequently, the choices available for the third voice are limited to those tones required to fulfill the predetermined intervalic relationships. (Note the skip of an augmented fourth—immediately resolved—in tones 1 and 2.)

By these rubrics, linear grace and interest are sacrificed to harmonic specifications—that is, chord structure and a more tonic-oriented root sequence. In principle this is the same compromise which was accepted along with eighteenth-century harmonic developments, and form is again shaped by statement of, departure from, and return to, the tonic.

9.24

In Example 9.25, the prevailing sound is the same as that in Example 9.24—m2, M3, m3. That basic sound is broken only at the upper climax (more tension) and in the cadence (a more stable interval, even though its root is not the tonic). Again, note the outlined triad in the second voice, this one also that of the dominant, enharmonically spelled.

9.25

*You may be tempted into a too-easy and too-frequent reliance on this compromise of triad outlines, to the detriment of linear freedom and grace. Don't succumb. Use it only when, after exhaustive effort, you can find no alternative.

Examples 9.26 and 9.27 offer two more prevailing sounds. The first uses only simple major and minor triads, while the other makes use of the tritone in combination with the major second. In sound, Example 9.26 approaches the Baroque and early Classical style. The identity is only superficial however, since only one stylistic factor is similar—the prevailing sound. Other factors, such as the treatment of chromatics and chord sequence, differ—particularly at the cadence.

9.26
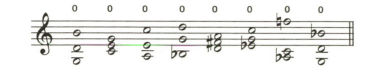

The tritone is so inveterately restless—particularly when not combined with another interval of unimpeachable stability, such as P5—that a string of them such as in Example 9.27 is apt to push the hearer toward tonal disorientation. Hence the need for scrupulous resolution is appropriately minimal in this sea of somewhat "free floating" sounds. In Example 9.27, however, each tritone is impeccably resolved—six of the nine to a member of the simple tonic triad. Nevertheless, the G-chord outlined at the close of the second voice is welcome in terms of tonic security.

9.27

Adherence to a prevailing sound is a virtual necessity in the achievement of a concentrated musical style. It need not be present in *every* combination of tones, but should clearly prevail at least to the extent that it does in Examples 9.20 to 9.22. The prevailing sound may be any interval or combination of intervals. There was a time when all music relied on P5 for this stylistic glue. At a later time it was the major and minor third. At the present time, when there is far less stylistic unanimity, a composer is free to employ anything which he can make convincing. Nevertheless, when in 1947 the critic Virgil Thompson wrote a series of articles about the replacement of *tertial* counterpoint by *secundal* counterpoint—the replacement of thirds by seconds—he had a cogent point.

The prevailing sound which we have been considering is, of course, only one of many stylistic determinants. But it is important, and perhaps the one most readily susceptible to mastery early in the game. In its further reaches, style is really a byproduct of a composer's maturing development.

10 COMPOSING A MINIATURE SUITE

ABOUT COMPOSING

The verb *to compose* means literally to put in place, or combine, various elements. To compose music would then mean to combine various sounds, presumably in a purposeful arrangement. This leaves open to the composer the choice of what sounds he is going to combine, how many or how few, and how to relate them to one another. The criteria for these choices are to a large extent determined by the musical mores of the time in which the composer lives—what is currently available and what the current taste is. Nowhere in the work of Palestrina, for instance, do the sounds of the sizzle cymbal and the electronic synthesizer appear, though it is quite possible that a composer of our own day might employ a minor triad or an a cappella choir. It would, however, be quite impractical for a composer of our day to call for the sound of the ophicleide or the serpent, instruments long since lost to general use.

The criteria determined by current taste are more subtle than those determined by availability. For example, all intervalic relationships between pitch frequencies theoretically have been available throughout the history of Western music, but only a limited number of these relationships were used in any given era. If Palestrina had suddenly taken it into his head to use some of the relationships with which you have been dealing, his opportunities for gainful employment would probably have diminished to the vanishing point. Conversely, at the time of J. S. Bach's death, his choices and purposes were no longer acceptable to the younger generation. Today it would be very difficult for a composer to attract a cultivated following if he habitually used pitch relationships any simpler than some of the more complicated ones which you have been using.

The era in which a composer lives also exerts a heavy influence on his choice of forms —the ways in which he combines his chosen materials. Fifteenth-century composers of polyphony, for example, loved to surround a plain chant with skillfully spun sonic embroidery. Repetitive song and dance forms were in high fashion during the eighteenth century—suite, sonata, passacaglia, da capo aria. By the turn of the nineteenth century no composer would have dreamed of neglecting to master the sonata-allegro form. The later nineteenth and early twentieth centuries reveled in musical forms dictated by literary content, such as the symphonic poem. A little later we witnessed the influence of a formal principle known as "continuous variation." And now, in our own day, the shape of many musical works is determined more, for instance, by "textures" and "densities" of sound than by motive, melody, tonal center, or even pitch relationships.

Likewise, different eras have demanded different uses for their music and therefore different aims of their composers. There have been times when entertainment—refined, vulgar, or both—was the primary goal. Other times have sought spiritual uplift or enlightenment, psychological revelation, sensuous titillation, intellectual stimulation, or nationalistic identification. Certain eras even seem to have placed the highest value on mere technical "correctness" on the one hand or on innovation at any cost on the other.

While composers generally have found it both expedient and "natural" to work within the musical mores of their own time, the more vigorous spirits among them have never felt bound by them. The inventive mind is never content to travel in the same way around the same grooves over and over again. Beethoven, for instance, certainly accepted almost unquestioningly the stylistic features employed by his contemporaries and immediate predecessors—scales, chord structure and sequence, formal conventions, etc. Yet from the very beginning there were constant touches which established him as an innovator—such things as well-placed rhythmic, dynamic, and harmonic surprises, and the rebalancing of formal proportions. Likewise, Stravinsky's *Rite of Spring,* considered wildly revolutionary in 1913, was in actuality quite conventional in strictly tonal matters—almost reactionary in the light of the incipient twelve-tone developments that were taking place in Vienna at the time. But in expressive aesthetic, in the exploitation of timbre, and in all rhythmic factors, *Rite* was a genuine trailblazer. Schoenberg's Suite for Piano, Op. 25 (1925), was another strong evolutionary force: for the first time, a twelve-tone row served as the basic tonal organizing force throughout an entire composition. Yet the aesthetic assumptions as well as the melodic gestures or motives were nineteenth century in origin, while the forms were borrowed from the eighteenth century. Other composers were immediately attracted to Schoenberg's method of composing with twelve tones, and by the mid-twentieth century it was the prevailing technique or style. But, as usual, composers had first refined it and had then begun bursting through its boundaries.

The truth of the above remarks is that though most composers inevitably accept whatever technical and musical habits and procedures they find, they do *not* compose by rule—not by the rules given in this text or in any other, past or present. Instead, they make the "rules"—insofar as whatever an inventive composer does in a thoroughly convincing manner becomes an integral part of the current and future body of musical resources, eventually turning up in those texts designed to train the student in the understanding and use of these resources.

Transition from the study of "theory" to composing is seldom easy even in the best of circumstances. The reason is that while the two are concerned with essentially the same materials, they are in actuality diametrically opposed to each other in approach. The first consists of the *analysis* and *assimilation* of handed-down procedures. The second is the *invention* of procedures and forms—incorporating, of course, whatever handed-down materials the composer may find useful. The transition is bound to be smoother and less painful if the student's theoretical work has stressed methods and materials related to the music of his own time. For the gifted fledgling composer that transition then involves only shifting from assimilation to invention—and, being gifted, he had probably formed a habit of invention long before he began his theoretical studies. On the other hand, if his theoretical training has stressed the old disciplines of harmony and counterpoint, then he is faced with the additional trauma of having to put aside a painstakingly acquired dead language and learning a new, live one. This can be devastating at a time when he should be free to address himself to composition itself rather than to mastering a new language— quite often even the very alphabet of that language.

Having mastered the use of the materials in this text up to this point, you are admirably equipped for the transition from assimilation to invention. This is not to imply that more than a small part of everything a composer needs to know is at your command—only that you can proceed to composition already equipped with the alphabet and a rudimentary vocabulary of today's musical language, together with a well-disciplined experience in choosing and controlling some of the smaller musical elements, such as tones, intervals, chords, tensions, and phrases.

And all potential musicians should try their hands at composition, regardless of whether or not they exhibit a special talent for it. For the performer and the historian there is no surer path to authoritative comprehension of a piece of music than speculation as to why it stands in its manifest form, what alternatives the composer might have rejected in a given situation, and even what compromises had to be made in order to achieve a con- centrated impact. And that speculation is necessarily whimsical and uninformed if the performer or historian cannot call upon *personal composing experience* to aid him in the process. Most of the greatest performers, past and present, have tried their hands at composing and always there are among us hundreds of young performers who achieve no more than mediocrity, not necessarily for lack of technical brilliance, but often through a lack of insight that this kind of experience might have remedied.

This book, of course, does not pretend to teach you composition. As an elementary text it attempts only to stretch your ears a bit, open a few windows, and sharpen your musical pencil. It is altogether fitting, however, that this final chapter should supply you with a little nudge in the direction of combining and meaningfully putting into place the various musical elements with which you have become acquainted through practical experience.

Perhaps you would be capable of a much broader leap into what is sometimes fatuously referred to as "free composition." For it is to be hoped that your work has fostered in you an enhanced sensitivity to the interaction of tones and intervals, both vertically and horizontally. It is also to be hoped that you have acquired some reliable habits of discrim- ination between logic and mere whim—and, similarly, between purpose and the mere memory of things repeatedly heard. The thoroughly experienced composer is prone to a high degree of reliance on these habits and sensitivities, and perhaps they would eventually carry you through to coherent expression. But you are not a thoroughly experienced composer. So I think you are apt to reach a degree of that coherent expression more quickly by proceeding step by step, taking care to ensure that certain basic principles are not disregarded.

THE FIRST PIECE

The Model and the Structures

We will begin, for illustration of method, by choosing a model (Ex. 10.1), on which our miniature suite for string trio will be based. This will serve as the model for several three-voice structures, which in turn will be placed one after the other. They will then be decorated or otherwise treated in such a way that each structure will furnish the guidelines for a phrase, more than one phrase, part of a phrase, or an entire section of a movement. The model will appear in any of the three voices, and sometimes it will be transposed to another tonal level. In one or two situations, it will be altered slightly to maintain the prevailing sound.

10.1

This procedure merely follows the time-honored principle of repeating—rather than constantly inventing—structural materials in the interest of formal unity. Examine carefully the full keyboard text of the Sarabande from Bach's English Suite No. 5 in E minor, whose melody you studied in Example 4.11. You will notice that, not only in melodic form but also in harmonic content and chord sequence, all the phrases show certain clear similarities to one another—with differences, to be sure. The same is true of the pieces shown in Examples 10.3, 10.5, 10.6, and 10.8, except that here we are using the three-voice structures rather than the eighteenth-century harmonic sequence to supply that kind of limitation by repetition. If you have string players in your class, rehearse the pieces until they can be played fluently. If you don't, try to find players elsewhere.

The first piece (Ex. 10.3) uses the techniques of decoration with which you have already become familiar. The underlying harmonic structure and the melodic guidelines are furnished by three three-voice structures of which the model (Ex. 10.1) serves as a unifying factor.

The first structure (Ex. 10.2a) is the same as in Example 9.24 (also the source of the model). The second structure (Ex. 10.2b) places the model in the upper voice and transposes it up a minor third. The third structure is a literal repetition of the first.

10.2

10.2

This ABA arrangement (statement, contrast, restatement) manifests, over the total decorated structure (Ex. 10.3), one of the first principles to be heeded when you began making models in Chapter 3—establishment of home, departure, and return home. It also exhibits, in principle, the skeleton on which the most common of all the old small forms were constructed.

Note also that the prevailing sound is maintained throughout, except for some variation by way of added and subtracted tension in the second structure. (This added tension again corroborates a principle to be found in the Bach Sarabande, for in that piece you will notice that in bars 13 and 14 the greatest amount of sustained harmonic tension, a diminished seventh chord, coincides with the maximum degree of motivic variation and reordering. This constitutes the tonal and melodic climax of the Sarabande.)

10.3   *The First Piece*

10.3

10.3

10.3

The Decoration

We will examine the decoration in Example 10.3 step by step.* Notice first that the chords of the three-voice structure are not given equal time in the decoration. A few minutes spent in careful comparison of the structures in Example 10.2a and b with the finished piece will reveal these differences. In general, a chord enjoys a comparatively long duration (five beats) when some principle, such as functional emphasis, seems to require it. If several adjacent chords are equal in duration, the intention is generally to establish a norm against which the effect of subsequent augmentations or diminutions can be heightened. Short chord durations (♩ or ♪) serve to draw attention to their functions by virtue of a noticeable change of pace. (See the B♭ chord in bar 9, third beat, and the half-beat durations allotted to chords 7, 8, and 9 of the second structure in bar 14 and again over the bar line from 15 to 16.) Notice also the two-beat chord durations in bars 18 and 19, giving way to three-beat durations in bars 20 and 21, followed by the five-beat duration of the antepenultimate chord in bars 22 and 23. This ritardation of harmonic rhythm serves to relax the pace as the piece nears its close, while the one-beat duration of the penultimate chord (bar 23, third beat) snaps the listener to attention for the final cadence.

In the melodic decorations, you will note that there are only two basic motives:

1. The semiarpeggiated one played by the violin in the first measure
2. The neighboring-tone figure in the same instrument's second bar

Phrase lengths vary somewhat in the violin part, which carries the principal melodic burden up to the beginning of bar 10. The first ends with the E♭ in bar 3, the second with

---

*In all these decorations, enharmonic spellings of many of the notes from the three-voice structures are freely used. This is in the interest of the clearest possible notation, to facilitate reading on the part of the instrumentalist.

the D♯ in bar 6, and the third with the C♯ in bar 9. The temporary cessation of rhythmic activity in the violin between its first and second phrases is bridged over by the cello, with its somewhat "flattened" version of motive 1. Otherwise the viola and cello give way to the melody in the violin, merely supplying harmonic and rhythmic support through exploitation of motive 2.

Note some of the binding forces employed at the climactic points in the melody of the violin part:

> Step-progression from G (bar 1) through A♭ (bar 4), high A♯ (bar 6), to the high B (bar 7)
> F (bar 1), E♭ (bar 3), to D (bar 4); low D♯ (bars 6 and 7), D, C, and B (bar 8), the B repeated (bar 9)

There are also meaningful step-progressions between this outer pair and throughout the rest of the piece. Find them.

In addition, motive 1 verges on service as a phrase head (page 50). Follow its course in the cello (bars 10 to 15) and through its variations in the violin (bar 16 to the end).

Take a look at bar 10. When the suspended B♭ in the cello resolves to A on the second sixteenth of the first beat, the final chord of the first three-voice structure is reached. With the upper A on the third beat, the chord is identical with the beginning of the second structure, except for C♯ in the violin. By thus replacing the C♮, the prevailing sound is maintained, an elision from the first to the second structure is effected, and the second section of the piece begins. In the process, the registral placement of the viola and cello has been reversed, with this color change enabling the cello to assume the melodic role in its upper register.

Throughout this second section, the violin, its activity reduced to a secondary role, maintains a gentle and steady, if minutely circuitous, upward climb to the A♭ in bar 14— in preparation for its much-elaborated reprise of the melody already heard in the first section. The second structure was planned to take advantage of the rising line of the model, with this very purpose in mind.

Notice what happens to the end of the second three-voice structure in bars 14 to 16. The last one and a half beats of bar 14 delineate chords 7, 8, and 9—except that the violin retains the A♭. The beginning of bar 15 would be the final chord of this structure except that the violin has not relinquished its A♭ and the cello has gone to A instead of E♭—a note which it never plays. The first chord of the returning first structure is reached on the second beat of bar 16, through a repetition of the last four chords of the second structure, the tones of the violin being telescoped, and the cello again substituting A for the E♭.

Study the last section carefully (bar 16 to the end). The variations on the original violin melody from section 1 are brought about by increasing the registral "sweep" of each gesture through octave displacement of some of the notes; by diminution (by half) of some of the rhythmic gestures; and by a kind of free invention in and surrounding the implementation of these two techniques. In the viola the neighboring-tone figure is maintained, but rather loosely, by the dual means of rhythmic displacement and skipping rather than stepping to and from the "neighbors"—rendering many of them, in fact, free tones rather than neighbors.

Careful analysis of Example 10.3 will reveal that the principle you have followed in your decorations of using only notes which will do no violence to the chord root has been generally followed. The principle has not been rigidly applied, however. Departures from it are usually in the interest of more compelling melodic direction, maintenance of prevailing sound, identity of motivic shape, etc. You will soon be composing at least one piece along the lines of Example 10.3, using the methods just discussed. When you do, try to keep uppermost in mind that you are now *composing,* and that, though you are doing it within the bounds of the musical principles set forth in this book, your ultimate aim is the invention of a coherent and even expressive piece of music rather than a mere demonstration of your mastery of the narrowest manifestations of those principles—the rules.*

Compose one or more little pieces using the techniques embodied in Example 10.3.

THE SECOND PIECE

The Structures

Example 10.5, the next piece to be examined, has as its skeleton another string of three-voice structures (Ex. 10.4a to f). Since its tempo is so fast that in no time flat its decoration would use up the three structures in Example 10.3, this piece employs *six* structures, two of them previously used in Example 10.3. In Example 10.4, you will note that (a) and (f) are identical, as were the first and last structures employed in Example 10.3. Also, (c) is identical to (a) and (f) except that it is transposed down a half-step or, to be completely accurate, up a major seventh. If you note some chromatic peculiarities in (d), just refer back to the same structure in Example 9.25, of which (d) is a transposition.

10.4

*If you wish to examine an older piece constructed on the same general principles as Example 10.3, look at the Air from Bach's Orchestral Suite No. 3 in D major. Though the harmonic sequences are eighteenth century, the principles of melodic construction, harmonic rhythm, phrase structure, and elision are strikingly similar.

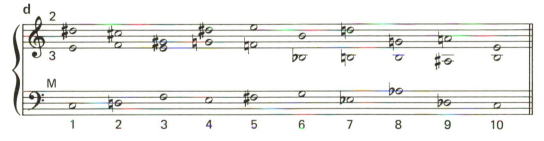

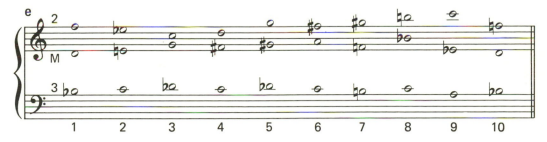

In Example 10.5, note that the prevailing sound of (a), m2, m3, M3—see Example 9.23—is maintained with only minor variations throughout all the structures except (e). There the prevailing sound, except in the first and last chords, is A4 and M2—slightly more tense than the others. This is only peripherally significant in this piece, but will assume more importance when we come to examine Examples 10.6 and 10.8.

10.5   *The Second Piece*

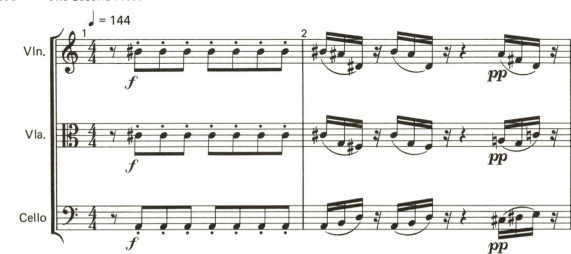

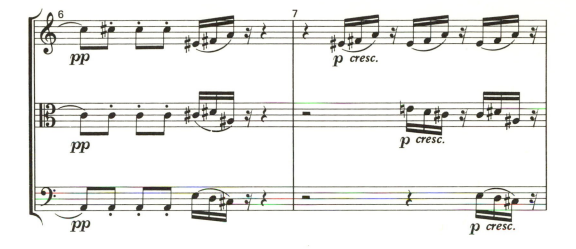

10.5

10.5

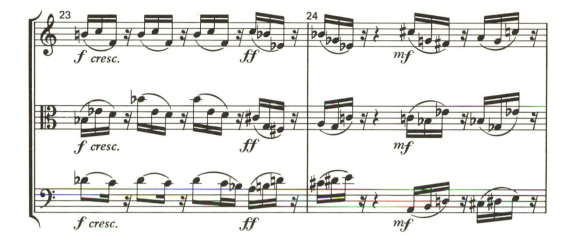

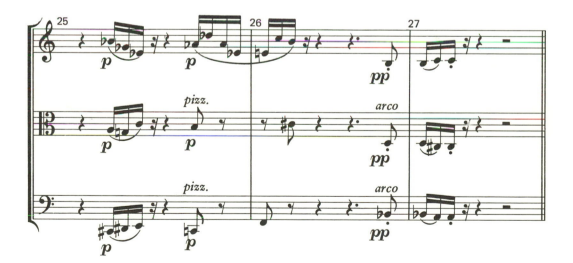

Rhythmic and Dynamic Exploitation

The term *decoration* as we have used it does not quite apply to Example 10.5, for the structures, in their skeletal function, are used in a different way. Chords and groups of chords (usually three) are merely exploited for rhythmic and dynamic purposes. After the sevenfold repetition of the first chord, the characteristic rhythmic motive (♪ ♪ ♪ 𝄾) at the beginning of bar 2 exploits the first three chords, repeating it on the second beat. The same motive on the fourth beat uses chords 4, 5, and 6. In the third bar, third and fourth beats, the same repeated motive repeats the same first six chords, going on to an augmentation of the motive in the fourth bar which uses chords 7, 8, and 9, with the final chord of (a) as a cadence on the third beat of that bar.

It is easy to see that after the last chord of (a) is repeated three times in bar 6, a similar process exploits the whole of (b) by the end of bar 9. Bars 1 to 5 and 6 to 9, then, represent complementary phrases which, together, form the first section of the piece.

Bar 10, ushering in the second section with a sharp contrast, begins the exploitation of (c). From the end of bar 12 to the middle of bar 15 the aim is clear—exploitation of the characteristic rhythmic motive and its augmentation, using the chords of (c) in groups of three as before, but in a slightly more legato style. In the middle of bar 15 the ends of the three voices of (c) are slightly staggered.

There follows a passage (middle of bar 15 to middle of bar 17) in which the notes of the last chord of (c) and those of the first chord of (d) are played with in such a way as to exploit the characteristic rhythmic motive, alter it a little, add to it, and maintain the prevailing sound of the piece. Though during this passage each of the instruments makes an attempt to get going with (d), that structure only really begins on the third beat of bar 17. Chords 4 to 9 of that structure are run through in hurricane fashion during the last half of bar 18—the climax of the piece. Structure (d) ends with the first beat of bar 19, though of course you will recognize the various repetitions which follow.

The slow passage played by the violin and viola in bars 20 and 21 is intended to round off the second section of the piece by recalling the somewhat similar passage in bars 10 to 12. E♭, D, E, and F at the beginning of bar 21 are borrowed from the beginning of (e) which, along with the final section of the piece, begins in earnest with the upbeat to bar 22, though the cello stays out until the second beat of that bar. Structure (e) comes to an end with the third beat of bar 23. Notice that the last three notes of the two upper parts are repeated three times in that bar. The cello, however, cheats a little by hammering away on the D♭ and C—virtually all it has done since bar 19 when these tones constituted its last two tones in (d). Poetic license!

The rest of the piece is pegged on (f). It remains only to say that though beats 3 and 4 of bar 24 constitute a repetition of the first six chords of that structure, the violin and viola exchange parts—with octave transpositions, of course. This switch not only freshens the sonority but also adds to the dichotomy between C and C♯ (D♭) which persists to the very last chord. (Such exchanges also took place in bars 13 and 14.) Note that the sixteenth-note passage in the violin beginning on the fourth beat of bar 25 constitutes *almost* (barring a couple of neighboring tones in bar 16) the only decoration in the sense that we have used the term up to now. That tiny passage serves as a sort of final gasp of surprise, sustaining interest to the very end.

> Exploiting the structures in this way may present a few challenges to your powers of invention, but try a piece or two using these methods.

THE THIRD PIECE

The Structures

Example 10.6 is constructed on the same sequence of three-voice structures as Example 10.5. And like the latter, it too employs virtually no tones other than those in the structures. In this way the two pieces differ radically from Example 10.3.

10.6   *The Third Piece*

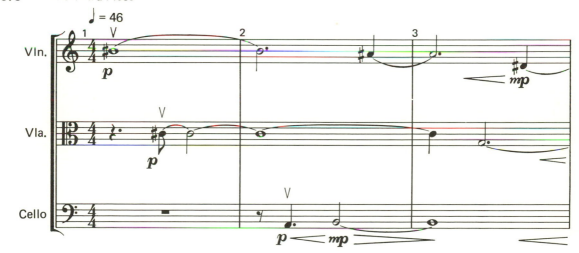

10.6

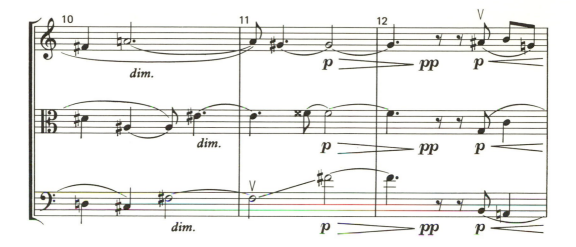

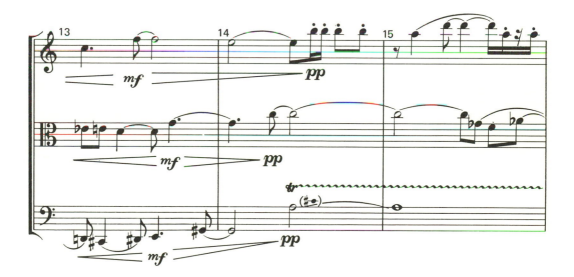

10.6

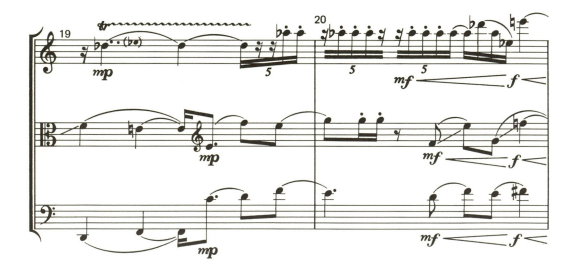

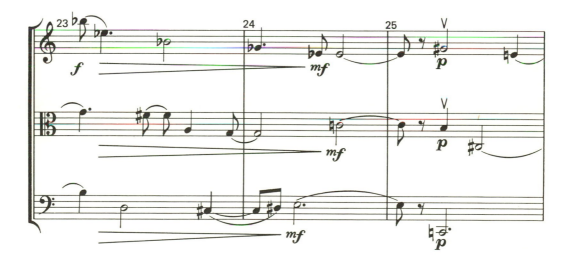

10.6

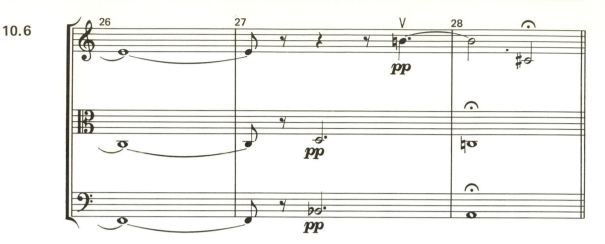

The shape of the piece is determined largely by rhythm which, in turn, is determined for the most part by the increasing and decreasing frequency of the attacks in the various instruments. Example 10.7 is a plot of the elapsed time between attacks. It covers the first 12½ bars of Example 10.6, with which you should compare it carefully. The first note in Example 10.7 represents the initial B♯ in the violin; its value indicates that 1½ beats elapse before the next attack in the viola C♯. Three full beats (♩ ♩ ♩ in Ex. 10.6) elapse before the next attack (♩.) in the cello (A), etc. The bars are marked merely for your convenience, and seldom coincide with attacks.

10.7

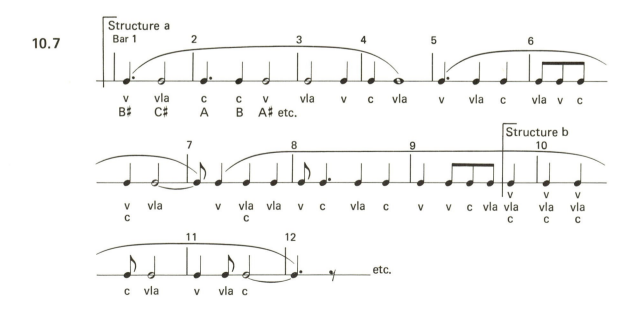

When your comparison is completed, look again at the plot. Notice that the rhythm, expressed through the irregularly spaced attacks, tends toward little waves of increasing and decreasing speed. The phrases, traditionally set off by cadences marked by momentary cessation of motion in melody, harmony, and rhythm, are here defined almost exclusively by cessation of rhythmic activity. Note that the phrase marks in the plot always lead to a comparatively long time lapse between attacks. Compare them with the phrase marks in Example 10.6.

Examine and analyze the rest of the piece for yourself, noting just how and where the general increase in speed takes place: it culminates in bar 21 with the fourteen consecutive thirty-second notes, and subsides from bar 22 to the end.

Pitch Exploitation

Now look back at the beginning of Example 10.6 to examine the method of pitch organization. It consists, of course, in exploiting each of the chords as they appear in the structures: you will notice that each group of three consecutive attacks spells out the next chord of the structure. Chord 1 is complete as soon as the cello plays its first tone, A. Chord 2 is completed with the viola's G in bar 3—etc. Since only one instrument moves at a time, and since all instruments are constantly sustaining their tones, many chords are formed which are not contained in the structure. And since each instrument plays only those tones which make up its horizontal line in the structure, choices must constantly be made as to which instrument should move next in order to maintain the prevailing sound —m2—and avoid intervals which would sound out of context in that prevailing sound, such as P5 and P4. For instance, once chord 1 was complete (cello A), it would have been un-desirable for the viola to move to its next tone, G, while the cello still sounded its A and the violin its B♯ (C), for the resulting chord would contain a P4 but no m2. So other choices were made which *do* maintain the m2 sonority. On the completion of chord 2 with the viola G, a search of the next structure chord reveals that there is no tone which would maintain the m2 sonority. So the D♯ is chosen (violin, bar 3), forming an aug-mented triad—the least offensive of three compromises.

Analyze for yourself how this general procedure is handled in the rest of the piece. In doing so, note how the last chord of (b) is elided in order to avoid disruption of the prevailing sound (middle of bar 13 on).

Note also how the structure chords as such are abandoned at times in favor of small fragments of the horizontal lines from the structures—always combined in such a way as to maintain the prevailing sound, barring one or two inconspicuous instances. This proce-dure begins unobtrusively in the middle of bar 12 (just the faintest hint of serialistic practice here). The various trills, introduced for their coloristic value, invariably exploit two tones which are horizontally adjacent in the structures.

Bar 21 was referred to above as a rhythmic culmination. For this reason, and also because of other factors—the intervalic tension in its first half and the high pitches in its second, for example—it is also the climax of the piece. Notice that as the speed slows down in bar 22, the structure being exploited is (e). Its increase in tension over the previous structures serves to sustain interest as the postclimactic denouement begins.

> Try composing a piece or two using the techniques employed in Example 10.6.

THE FOURTH PIECE

The Structures

The structures underlying Example 10.8 are all among those in Example 10.4. They are:

Structure (a)
Structure (b)—transposed up an A4
Structure (a)—transposed up an M2
Structure (b)—transposed down an M2
Structure (e)
Structure (e)—transposed up a P5
Structure (a)

10.8   *The Fourth Piece*

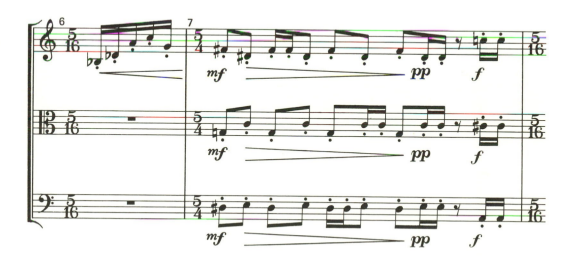

10.8

10.8

10.8

10.8

Textural Exploitation

The constructive formula of the piece is the alternation of two contrasting textures:

    Staccato—bars 1 to 12
    Legato—bars 13 to 17
    Staccato—bars 18 to 24
    Legato—bars 25 to 29
    Staccato—bars 30 to 40

Scattered through the staccato sections and always "framing" the legato sections are the little interpolated asymmetrical bars with a sixteenth-note pulse which break up the otherwise rigid quarter-note pulse of the staccato sections. These bars first increase and then decrease in length as the piece progresses: 5/16, 5/16, 5/16, 7/16, 7/16, 9/16, 7/16, 5/16, 3/16, 3/16, 3/16. Except in one instance, bar 8, these interpolated bars are in no way derived from the structure chords as decoration. They do, however, preserve the basic sound relationship in that they arpeggiate the type of chord that forms the prevailing sound—m2, m3, M3.

The two legato sections also tend to break up, and contrast with, the rigid prevailing quarter note pulse, because in these sections the rhythmic unit in at least one of the instruments, sometimes two, sometimes all three, is the dotted eighth.

The specific use of the structure chords in this piece will be just a bit more difficult to follow than in the others because, while all of the tones are almost invariably present, they are not always played by the "proper" instrument. The first two chords of (a) merely oscillate back and forth throughout bars 1 and 2. In the first half of bar 4, chord 3 is heard but the viola plays D♯ instead of its "proper" D, while the violin plays D instead of D♯. Note the free tones—the second of each pair of sixteenths.

The chord at the end of bar 4 is chord 4, rearranged and with D♯ (E♭) held over from the previous chord. These rearrangements are always for the purpose of achieving the desired sonority in each case. How does the composer decide what the desired sonority is? He experiments—and he uses his imagination.

Bar 8 with its upbeat recapitulates the first six chords of (a). The chord in bar 9 is chord 7 of (a), again with E♭ (D♯) held over from the previous chord. Bar 11 finishes off the first structure with an oscillation between chords 9 and 10, rearranged, respelled, and recalling the procedure of bars 1 and 2, rounding out the first section of the piece.

The first contrasting legato section, with some repetition of two- and three-note groups and a couple of omissions as well as other adjustments, is built on (b), transposed a tritone, and followed by (a), transposed up a major second. In bar 18, note the many repetitions of the tones of the first two chords of (b), here transposed down a major second. The last chord in bar 23 contains the two tones of the last chord of (b) (transposed, you remember), but with the C♯ (D♭) held over from the previous chord in order to retain the prevailing sound and lead to the 9/16 bar.

With some elision by way of omission (to avoid an ill-placed violation of the prevailing sound) the second legato section uses (e) followed by its own transposition up a perfect fifth. Bar 32 contains a matter of some interest. Chord 3 of (a), which began with bar 30, consists of the D♯ in the violin (first beat) plus the D in the cello and the F♯ in the violin (second half of first beat). The remaining three notes of the five-tone chord are the three tones of chord 4. The five-part chord heard on the second half of beat 3 in this bar contains the five tones yielded by chords 5 and 6 of the structure. Chord 6 is repeated by itself at the beginning of bar 34—then on to chord 7 and to the end of the structure and the piece.

Compose a piece using the technical procedures employed in Example 10.8.

To conclude our examination of the four pieces in this little suite, it should be pointed out that for performance purposes the order should be Examples 10.6, 10.8, 10.3, and 10.5. Played in this sequence they present sufficient contrast from piece to piece to maintain interest—contrast in tempo, type of musical idea, harmonic and melodic exploitation, and aesthetic aura. Unity, on the other hand, is maintained through the constant use of the same model even while different structures are built on it. Unity is further served by the consistent presence in each piece of the same prevailing sound. Unity is perhaps even overworked since in all the pieces the tone A serves as tonal center, tenuous as that tonal center may seem at times.

FINAL REMARKS

This book has fulfilled its aims, and will take you no further than this point into the art of composition. If you yourself choose to explore this field further, and I hope you will, you will no doubt find a composition class open to you. In that class your techniques as well as your aims will be greatly expanded. You may begin to explore more of the specific techniques of the recent past, such as extended tonality, pandiatonicism, polyfunctionalism, polytonality, and the all-important serialistic techniques. It is to be hoped that in your composition class you will also become acquainted with at least some of the techniques that have emerged in recent years, such as aleatoric methods, diversified timbral combinations, methods which minimize the importance of precise pitch, the pulverization of pulse as well as the exploitation of conflicting pulses, and the use of microtones.

Form is another factor you should study assiduously. To imitate the formulas of the past is very easy. It is a far more challenging thing to view form as the basic shape (including psychological impact) which you conceive for your piece, and to find fresh means by which to delineate that shape.

A whole world of wonder will open to you if you plan to go beyond the limits of the materials of this book. I wish you luck—and joy.

APPENDIX 1
A Checklist of Rules

The following brief digest of the rules in Chapters 3, 5, and 7 is intended for quick and easy reference only. Not all exceptions are listed. When in doubt, refer to the text on the page given.

Chapter 3

1. The length of the model is never less than seven and seldom more than twelve tones (18).
2. The range of the model seldom exceeds an octave by more than one tone (18).
3. The model begins and ends on the same tone in the same octave and avoids intervening emphasis on that tone (18-19).
4. The final tone may be approached by whole- or half-step or any interval skip, no larger than P5, of which the last tone is the root (19).
5. Melodic progressions are limited to perfect, major, and minor intervals, none larger than P5 (20).
6. If an augmented or diminished interval should appear as tones 1 and 3 of any three-note group, tone 2 must be the half-step resolution of tone 1 (21; *exceptions:* 22).
7. The first member of A1, A8, or d8 must resolve at some point *before* the second member may appear, regardless of the number of intervening tones (22-23).
8. Avoid repeating a tone without intervening skips strong enough to deemphasize the repetition (24-25).
9. Avoid outlined triads without a passing tone *and* a change of direction (25).
10. Avoid scalar passages of more than three tones. Change direction before and after each three-tone scalar passage (25).
11. Avoid sequences (26).
12. Be careful of melodic contour in regard to climaxes, and never repeat a climax tone (28).
13. Avoid more than four tones without a change of direction (29).

14. Avoid skips larger than P5. One step in the same direction on either side, or both sides, of P5 is permitted (29).
15. Avoid adjacent skips in the same direction (29).

Chapter 5

16. Melodic requirements for the second voice are the same as for the model, except:
    a. The final note may be approached by any permissible melodic progression (71).
    b. The second voice need not begin and end on the same note unless it is below the model, in which case it must (71).
17. The root of the last interval must be in the lower voice (71).
18. Avoid repeated tones except under certain conditions (72).
19. All intervals of tension are to be immediately resolved (72).
20. The voices may not cross (73).
21. Only one of the voices may skip in the final progression (74).
22. Avoid parallel perfect intervals, even in contrary motion (74).
23. Avoid simultaneous skips in similar or parallel motion (75).
24. Avoid coincidental melodic climaxes (75).
25. Avoid progressions in which *all four* tones add up to a simple triad or a seventh chord which contains a tritone (76).
26. Avoid progressions containing exclusively M2, M3, and A4 (77).
27. Be careful of adjacent vertical intervals with ambiguous roots (77).
28. Avoid the immediate anticipation of any tone of the lower voice *in the same octave* (78).
29. Avoid covered perfect intervals in which the upper voice skips upward (79).
30. Avoid covered octaves except at the cadence (80)—but see rule 29.
31. Progressions approaching *and* leaving P4 must include at least one stepwise voice (81).
32. If one member of A1, A8, or d8 appears alone in either voice, its resolution must occur *in the same voice* before, or simultaneously with, the introduction of the other member *in either voice* (81).

Chapter 7

33. Avoid voice crossings (123).
34. Avoid coincidental melodic climaxes (123).
35. Melodic requirements for the third voice are the same as for the model, except:
    a. The first and last tones need not be the same unless the third voice is on the bottom (123).
    b. The last tone may be approached by any melodically permissible interval (123).
    c. Tones may be repeated (123).
    d. The direction need not change after four tones (123).
    e. Scalar passages are permitted (123).
36. All tensions must be immediately resolved (124).
37. The root of the last chord must be in the lower voice (125).

38. Avoid covered P1 or P8, except at the cadence, and even then do not approach its upper tone by upward skip (126).
39. The six tones contained in any progression should not add up to a seventh chord containing a tritone (126).
40. Never double an active tone and, except at the cadence, avoid other doublings (127). If it is *impossible* to avoid the latter, the best doublings are:
    a. Tonic, dominant, or subdominant
    b. The root of any chord—(a) and (b) might coincide
41. Any but the outer voices may skip simultaneously in the same direction (127)—but see rule 42.
42. Every progression should contain at least one stepwise voice (127)—but see rule 43.
43. If all voices *must* skip, there can be no doubling (127).
44. Covered P5 or P4 with the upper voice skipping upward is permitted between any but the outer voices *if* there are no doublings in the progression (127).
45. Avoid parallel perfect intervals except stepwise parallel perfect fourths between the upper voices, and then *only* if there are no doublings (127).
46. Avoid the immediate anticipation of any tone of the lower voice in the same octave (127).
47. Avoid chords with roots a perfect fourth above the bass unless:
    a. The bass moves through stepwise (127).
    b. The bass remains stationary (127).
48. Treat A1, A8, and d8 precisely as in the two-voice structure (128)—and see rule 32.

APPENDIX 2
Suggested Listening

The idea behind this list is more important than any particular item on it: the list is so arranged that the student hears an old and a new work each week until the works converge in time around the turn of the twentieth century. With this arrangement, no nineteenth-century work appears until late in the list, a fact that will broaden the listening experience of the many incoming college students who have been exposed to little else.

These assignments and the works included in any week are entirely optional. Instructors may wish to make other choices, depending on what recordings are available to their classes and what recordings—particularly of other new works—are subsequently issued.

First week
  Krzysztof Penderecki: *Threnody for the Victims of Hiroshima*
  Guillaume de Machaut: Mass: Notre-Dame

Second week
  Earle Brown: *Available Forms I*
  Orlandus Lassus: Madrigals (any half dozen)

Third week
  Pierre Boulez: *Marteau sans maître*
  Giovanni Palestrina: *Missa Papae Marcelli*

Fourth week
  Luciano Berio: *Sinfonia*
  Giovanni Gabrieli: *Canzoni* (for brass choirs)

Fifth week
  Morton Subotnick: *Touch*
  Carlo Gesualdo: *Dolcissima mia vita*

Sixth week
  John Cage: *Fontana Mix*
  Claudio Monteverdi: *Cantate Domino*

Seventh week
  Iannis Xenakis: *Eonta*
  Heinrich Schütz: *St. John Passion*

Eighth week
  George Crumb: *Ancient Voices of Children*
  Joseph Haydn: *The Creation*

Ninth week
  Charles Whittenberg: *Triptych for Brass Quintet*
  Antonio Vivaldi: *The Seasons*

Tenth week
  Alvin Etler: Quintet for Brass Instruments
  J. S. Bach: Brandenburg Concerto No. 4

Eleventh week
  Elliott Carter: String Quartet No. 2
  G. F. Handel: *Water Music*

Twelfth week
  Karlheinz Stockhausen: *Refrain; Zyklus*
  Henry Purcell: *Dido and Aeneas*

Thirteenth week
  Olivier Messiaen: *Quatuor pour le fin du temps*
  J. S. Bach: Mass in B minor

Fourteenth week
  Karlheinz Stockhausen: *Gesang der Jünglinge*
  Domenico Scarlatti: Sonatas for harpsichord (any half dozen)

Fifteenth week
Jacob Druckman: *Incenters*
Joseph Haydn: Symphony No. 101
("Clock")

Sixteenth week
Igor Stravinsky: *Agon*
Joseph Haydn: String quartets, Op. 76
(any one)

Seventeenth week
Alban Berg: *Lyric Suite*
W. A. Mozart: *Don Giovanni*

Eighteenth week
Edgard Varèse: *Octandre*
W. A. Mozart: Symphony No. 41 ("Jupiter")

Nineteenth week
Béla Bartók: *Music for Strings, Percussion, and Celesta*
Ludwig van Beethoven: String Quartet, Op. 95

Twentieth week
Arnold Schoenberg: String Quartet No. 4
Franz Schubert: Mass in G major

Twenty-first week
Arnold Schoenberg: Suite for Piano, Op. 25
Ludwig van Beethoven: Symphony No. 7

Twenty-second week
Béla Bartók: String Quartet No. 4
W. A. Mozart: Piano Concerto No. 20, D minor

Twenty-third week
Paul Hindemith: Kleine Kammermusik, Op. 24, No. 2
Ludwig van Beethoven: Symphony No. 3 ("Eroica")

Twenty-fourth week
Anton Webern: *Cantata No. 1*
Hector Berlioz: *L'Enfance du Christ*

Twenty-fifth week
Edgard Varèse: *Poème électronique*
Felix Mendelssohn: Symphony No. 3 ("Scotch")

Twenty-sixth week
Aaron Copland: Piano Variations
Robert Schumann: Symphony No. 3 ("Rhenish")

Twenty-seventh week
Anton Webern: Variations for Piano, Op. 27
Richard Wagner: *Tristan und Isolde:* "Prelude" and "Liebestod"

Twenty-eighth week
Igor Stravinsky: *The Rite of Spring*
Johannes Brahms: Symphony No. 2

Twenty-ninth week
Arnold Schoenberg: *Pierrot Lunaire*
Richard Strauss: *Don Juan*

Thirtieth week
Charles Ives: String Quartet No. 2
Claude Debussy: *Nocturnes*

INDEX